The Presence Driven Leader

A Handbook for the 21st Century Echelon Leader

The
PRESENCE
DRIVEN
Leader

Dr. Mark E. Kauffman

Forewords by Dr. William Hinn & Bishop Tommy Reid

The **PRESENCE DRIVEN** *Leader*

A Handbook for the 21st Century Echelon Leader

Printed in the USA

ISBN (Print): 978-0-9995055-0-2

ISBN (Kindle): 978-0-9995055-1-9

LCCN (Library of Congress Control Number): 2017915668

Unless otherwise noted, scripture references are taken from the King James Version of the Bible. The King James Version is public domain in the United States.

Scripture quotations taken from the Amplified® Bible are marked AMP. Copyright © 2015 by The Lockman Foundation. Used by permission. www.Lockman.org.

To contact the author:

thepresencedrivenlife.com

Dedication

I dedicate this book to my lovely wife and companion in the faith, Jill. I'm honored to walk with you on this incredible journey that together we call the Presence driven life.

To my beloved son, Christian Mark, may the footsteps I follow lead you into a greater Presence driven life than I will ever experience.

This book is also dedicated to every Presence driven leader who is impregnated with divine purpose and who is passionate to see the Presence of the Lord established in the lives of their followers. May the words penned within this book inspire you to be a Presence driven leader!

Praise for The Presence Driven Leader

Mark Kauffman is an amazing man and an uncommon leader. My appreciation and admiration of him transcends his work and the scope of ministerial obligations, to his value as a man that the urgency of our times demands. In comparison, his endeavors and achievements surpass the nominal responsibilities which qualify one for the levels of civil servant, community leader, and yes, even the Congress.

Mark is a modern-day leader carved out from an ancient mold. He therefore bears the evidence of proving, polishing, and presentation of consistent integrity, unmitigated commitment, and the rare quality of a desire to elevate others to his levels of success and accomplishments. Dr. Kauffman's interest is not to be a pied piper desiring the profane adulations of purposeless followers, nor has he been a self-seeking servile flatterer tooting his own horn of affluence. Rather, he is as a ram caught in the thicket of destiny's grill, he comes to the slaughter with intention to give his life to his grossly failing generation and "he would not …" He would not make professional excuses which has become blasé in political circles, he would not abort his duty for temporary gain and pleasure, he would not exempt the intimacy of his family from the higher call of which wind he has caught, he would not color one image to those impressed by him and later reveal a disguised face of deception to those seeking truth. Finally, he would not pervert what is true, but purify, clarify, and qualify the truth to others.

A prominent quality among those who are leaders to other leaders is that of multi-tasking. This is Mark's forte. Every plant evades the swamp, yet there the lily makes its home. Massive trees thin out and do not blossom as they reach their altitude, yet there the eagle makes its nest. The desert scorches, burns, and buries every living organism, yet there the cactus takes advantage of certain barrenness and bears a sap which is harvested for the world. Fully grown it can carry 750 liters of water (in the desert). The tumbleweed viewed as wilderness trash, climbs into a desert wind as its Rolls Royce and travels hundreds of miles spreading seeds of new life as it goes.

I have been there with this man through some of his fiercest battles, but there as the lily he shines. I watched as some close ones forsook him and walked away, but instead of being bitter toward them, he rose above the fray and flew higher. For several years, recently, he stood his greatest test as his baby boy was afflicted with a rare illness. Yet as the cactus, he gathered the water of life to quench the thirst of other afflicted ones. And forgive my indulgence, but the very few times when as men we shared tears together, he was usually in his car and like the tumble weed, flying down the highway to his next mission, to help save someone's marriage, or prevent an organization from going under, or to turn a leader back from the folly of his ways.

Professionalism, skill sets, marketability and good work ethics are the lesser of what's required for great leadership. The weightier requirement being a distinct call to serve; a dedicated life of sacrifice; a true desire to see others not "as trees walking" (decorations of our individual successes); and conclusively, the distant, consistent sound of destiny's voice, for if we are driven and not led this spells disaster.

There must be a Presence which both pulls and propels Dr. Kauffman to his work and to this end, he makes it so easy.

This handbook is long overdue, not for those who aspire to leadership by rote, but for those whose right it is and who have answered the call to live while dying daily.

—DR. CARL C. ALEXANDER
Bishop, Senior & Founding Pastor of Tabernacle of Praise for all Nations
www.carlalexanderministries.com

I highly recommend Dr. Mark's book, *The Presence Driven Leader,* to those who have an ear to hear and a desire to lead. His insight is worth the time and funds to increase your knowledge. This book has been incredibly written, a life-driven insight into a subject needed by many.

—DR. RON DEPRIEST
President and Founder of Ron DePriest Ministries
www.rondepriest.com

This book is indeed what it claims to be, a *Handbook for the 21st Century Echelon Leader*. Dr. Mark E. Kauffan's work is refreshing, authentic, inspirational, and practical!

As a true sent one in the marketplace, he has become the message and ergo, propagates the ancient truths of God's Word in a palpable and authoritative manner. It would serve the reader of this literary gem well to consider thc life essence poured into the enriching quotes offered. This publication reveals Mark's discovery of God's light and eternal truths on his path, through many episodes of personal trials and tribulations.

Over the years of knowing him as a beloved brother, friend, and a herald of truth, I have seen how he has owned up to the requirement of our Father towards an accurate Word and Spirit alignment. When the going got tough, the Christ in Mark got tougher!

His sincere passion and drive to bring Christ's life as victorious Conqueror to God's people—bringing heaven to earth—is contagious and commendable.

This treatise will illuminate the path of the pilgrim whose heart is set on migration towards Zion. It will encourage, embolden, and enrich you in more ways than you can imagine.

Therefore, I do not only laud this handbook as a praiseworthy accomplishment, but also highly recommend its assimilation into the minds of those who hunger and thirst for God's righteous ways

For, in truth, *"Blessed are they which do hunger and thirst after righteousness, for they shall be filled"* (Matthew 5:6).

The Presence Driven Leader not only carries my enthusiastic endorsement, but also sincere hope that it would, as a transformative acquisition to your library, bring great light, joy, and encouragement to you.

—BEN KLEYNHANS, Ph.D
Founder of Touch the Nations Ministries
www.ttn.co.za

My friend and apostolic colleague, Dr. Mark Kauffman, has a rare combination and gifting of wisdom, discernment, revelation, communication, motivation, vision, integrity, character, and leadership. He has greatly blessed the world by penning this literary masterpiece worth its weight in gold. In this power-packed book, *The Presence Driven Leader,* Dr. Kauffman has designed and delivered to us a robust treasury and storehouse of distilled wisdom. So, it is no surprise that this connoisseur and expositor par excellence of God's Word, has assembled arguably one of the most potent and valuable arsenals of spiritual munitions, weapons, and principles ever conceived. Dr. Kauffman, in his desire to pass on what he has learned and mastered in life to others, has created over 700 of the most powerful leadership quotes ever written and added to them his insights, comments, and wisdom from decades of senior leadership experience in both the marketplace and the church. When Dr. Mark speaks, people listen—you should, too. If you will read and apply this divine wisdom, your life will never be the same.

—**DR. BRUCE COOK**
Author, Speaker, Consultant, Publisher, Investor Board Chair, KCIA
www.kcialliance.org

Dr. Mark Kauffman thinks, speaks, preaches, believes, and lives his life as a Presence driven leader! He is what he so passionately writes about. He is the embodiment of his message. In this book, he writes with clear understanding about echelon Presence driven leadership and leading the present-day church into "Greater Glory" of the Kingdom restoration and reformation.

The Presence Driven Leader discusses recovering, restoring, and transforming the church from its "weekend church services" mentality to an aggressive everyday marketplace; not giving in to the ownership of the culture and the economics of the present world system, but rather possessing and leading this world into the greater light of the Kingdom of God!

We must not abandon the earth, acting as though we can't do anything to change it. We have done that far too long. We desperately need a rising army of Presence driven leaders who will not only change this world, but also rule the forces of darkness in our cities. Dr. Mark will show you how that can be accomplished.

If that message captures your heart, this book will take you there. Most of all, you will come to know the Presence of the Holy One that my friend knows so well. Like no one else I know, he is "… a man with a different spirit." If you apply what he shares, you will be also.

—**PAUL BERSCHE**
Pastor, Author, Teacher
www.paulberscheministries.com

Many manuscripts cross my desk each year. It is my privilege to assist authors polish and publish their work. I treasure each one as a unique expression of God breathing life into their pages. Few, however, capture me as *The Presence Driven Leader* has. My heart beats to this same rhythm: excellence, service, preparation, character, favor … it was like I was reading my own words. My spirit vibrated in resonance to the frequency of heaven coming through the phrases which so clearly represent the heart of the one who penned them.

Dr. Mark's quotes are pithy and powerful. They are memorable and deliver truth in a unique way. Helping bring this project forth has been an honor. This is a resource I will refer to often and recommend even more. *The Presence Driven Leader* is not a call to be famous or even effective, it is a call to pour out your life as a beautiful offering to the One who fashioned you before earth's foundation was ever formed. Hear the call and come up higher.

—**WENDY K. WALTERS**
Motivational Speaker, Branding & Publishing Expert, Director of The Favor Foundation
www.wendykwalters.com

Acknowledgements

First and foremost, I thank the Holy Spirit, my teacher
who has guided me into the Presence driven life.

I wish to thank Jill, my wife, for the continual encouragement and
love that you have expressed toward me throughout our 28 years
of marriage and while I wrote this brook. Your Presence driven
life has provoked me to pursue His Presence more fervently.

To Christian Mark, Anthony, and Ryan—my three beloved
sons—many of the quotes penned in this book are a result
of the wonderful privilege I have had to be your father and
to raise you in the fear and admonition of the Lord.

To the Jubilee Ministries family who have given your lives in
service to the Lord Jesus Christ and the Kauffman family.

To Tanya Patxot, Carrie Johnson, Kim Taylor,
Michelle Cummings, and Belinda Wright for
your help editing and organizing this book.

To Dr. William Hinn, my spiritual father and mentor,
I honor you and thank you for being the example of
a man who lives as a Presence driven leader.

To all the men and women who have influenced me and helped me to believe I am who God said I was: Bishop Tommy Reid, Dr. Carl Alexander, Dr. Kelley Varner, Dr. Ron DePriest, Apostle Frans DuPlessis, and Dr. Steven Everett, just to name a few. I salute you and thank you for taking the time to invest in me.

Last but not least, to Kenneth and Rosemary Kauffman, my parents, thank you for leading us by example into a Presence driven life.

Foreword by
Dr. William Hinn

For at least the last few decades, the Spirit of God has been raising, developing, pruning and refining a new breed of leaders who are driven by the hunger to reveal the reality of Jesus Christ and the excellency of His kingdom.

"But the end and culmination of all things has now come near; keep sound-minded and self-restrained and alert therefore for (the practice of) prayer" (1 Peter 4:7, AMP). The word "culmination" means, to reach the highest point or degree, the climactic condition. Everything in God works in cycles of divine activity—as one cycle comes to a close another one begins. At the highest point of the cycle is the most intense activity of change. We are now in one of the most intense transformations in church history.

I believe the Lord is now releasing a pioneering spirit in His chosen men and women, leaders who carry the heavenly blueprint of building and releasing the revelation of the Kingdom of God into their territories and regions. With apostolic wisdom, they will embrace covenant relationships versus competitions and finally, raise a unified body that will release the power of the kingdom like this world has never seen. Their Christ-like lives will create a new environment, breaking the limitations and restrictions that are controlling the people of God, that will pave the way and usher in the greatest unveiling of Christ in human flesh!

It is my conviction that Dr. Mark Kauffman personifies *The Presence Driven Leader.* His life exemplifies the heart, motive, and selfless drive of our Lord Jesus Christ. This book will enlighten, encourage, confirm and awaken the vision of the Father in the hearts of His sons. It will point them back to the original plan and purpose of God when He said, "Let us make man in our image"— it is this man—the image of God man that Dr. Mark Kauffman is calling out, the Presence driven leader!

—DR. WILLIAM HINN
Founder & Senior Pastor of Resurrection Life Center

Foreword by
Bishop Tommy Reid

I have awaited with bated breath for Mark to tell me when he was going to write a book for and to leaders. Apostle Mark, the world has been waiting for this moment.

I knew that when my friend, Mark Kauffman, would write a book to leaders, it would be one of the greatest books on leadership that has ever been written. I have watched his skills of leadership with amazement and wanted to beg him to write a book about the qualities of leadership he exhibited. So, before I ever read a word, I knew it was great, and perhaps the best leadership guide ever penned, but then I am prejudiced.

Prejudiced, because I have known so many great leaders. I have known some of the great leaders of the past 80 years. I was a close personal friend and served as member and the Executive Secretary of Robert Schuller's board of Churches Uniting in Global Mission. I was a close friend of Oral Roberts, and for a season he asked me to serve as the Chairman of his financial committee. Lester Sumrall was my mentor, and I spent long hours as he discipled me as a young preacher. I have known great leaders, but Mark Kauffman stands the tallest of any leader I have ever met. So, I knew this would be a great book. And never before have I ever seen nearly

700 quotes for leadership assembled in one resource .... that alone is more than worth the price of this book.

The greatest thing about this book is that you will become intimate with its author. You will read and get to know the greatness of this leader. You will learn why he values the "Presence of God" with the same passion as Moses when he said, "If Your Presence does not go with us, we do not want to go." The Presence of God is greater than any destination or realization of success. One cannot be around Mark Kauffman without discovering that his great success is because of the journey he is taking into the Presence of God.

> **The Presence of God is greater than any destination or realization of success**

Secondly, you will discover Mark's formula for success. I have always found that knowing a leader is wonderful, but getting to know the secret that has made them successful and great is the most productive journey in the world. This time, you will not only read the wise words of the successful leader who wrote the book, but you will get inside of his spirit. And when you do, you will find Christ. He is a man who understands that he thinks like Christ, because he has the mind of Christ. He is a man who does the things that the Father wants done on the earth, because he has the arms and hands of Christ. He is a man who has an intimate relationship with Jesus, because he has felt His emotion and loves the things that Jesus loves.

As great as the information that Mark Kauffman has to share with you, most of all he will literally "share Mark Kauffman" with the reader. You will get to know him, and like myself, you will discover true greatness.

So, take the journey with me into the life of one of the truly great leaders of the world, but fasten your seat belt, you will never be the same again.

When I was a child I used to say to my friend, Lorne, "I dare you to do that," and then I would add, "No Lorne, I DOUBLE DARE YOU TO DO THAT."

So, take my advice, "I double dare you to read this!" ... you will never be the same again.

—BISHOP TOMMY REID

Author of *The Exploding Church, How to Live Out of a Dream, Kingdom Now But Not Yet,* and *Create Wealth to Build God's Dreams*

www.tommyreid.org

Introduction

The Lord is creating a new wineskin to facilitate the 21st Century church—to be the true salt and light Jesus called us to be. We must now become a wall-less church that influences society.

Man was created for Kingdom conquest (Genesis 1:26-28). When the Kingdom of God is only a Sunday event, man's need and passion for conquest is misplaced. When men and women in the marketplace do not have a clear vision regarding their callings and assignments, their need for conquest will be misdirected. Misplaced conquest always leads to sinful and unproductive lifestyles. When King David was called to be on the battlefield he was found in the bedroom, this is misplaced conquest.

The true battle in this hour is in the marketplace, or what we call the 7 Mountains of society: Family, Church, Media, Government, Education, Arts/Entertainment, and Finance/Business (Isaiah 2:2). As Presence driven leaders we are called to recover and restore the earth for God and bring it under His Kingdom rule. This book was written for the purpose of empowering, equipping, and preparing Presence driven leaders to influence, transform, and lead the 21st Century Kingdom Reformation.

Presence driven leaders are chosen by the Lord and called to be kings and priests unto our God, manifesting Him in every sphere of society (Revelation 1:6). As priests in the marketplace, we create atmospheres and minister to everyone in our sphere—pray for them, heal them, prophesy into their purpose, encourage them, and lead them into an intimate Presence driven life with Jesus Christ. As kings, we are to rule over every circumstance, take dominion over principalities and powers that keep our cities and people captive, and establish a Kingdom culture in the sphere the Lord has called us to (Luke 10:19). Our pursuit as Presence driven leaders in the marketplace is not just revival, but the establishment of Christ's Kingdom in the planet.

The church has had programs, revivals, and healing campaigns, yet we have not brought deliverance to creation. We have never brought a permanent change by transforming atmospheres over our cities with Christ's Kingdom culture. As Presence driven leaders, we are to occupy the territory we are assigned to in His glorious name and rule in His stead (Luke 19:13).

New birth is not merely a means to keep you from hell's flames and give you admission to heaven, but to restore man to his rightful place in the earth as kings and priests. It is to bring eternal change to our world, and reshape history as we know it for the glory of God. It has never been God's purpose and intent to evacuate us from the planet, but to recover it, bring it under the Lord's leadership, and fill it with His glory. It has never been God's plan to take us out of the earth, but to take over the earth and colonize it with a new Kingdom culture

The meek shall inherit the earth.

MATTHEW 5:5

The current war we face in our world is for culture and economics. The Kingdom of God is more than evangelism, deliverance, and salvation. It is to recover, reform, and refill the earth with Christ's Kingdom (Matthew 28:18-20). Kingdom reformation and restoration are the only answer to the world's current chaos.

Kingdom reformation and restoration are the only answer to the world's current chaos

God's purpose and plan has never changed for mankind. It has always been to create man in His likeness and image, and to bless them that they might be fruitful, multiply, and replenish the earth, subdue it, and have dominion (Genesis 1:27-28). This is the mandate upon Presence driven leaders.

God is after the recovery of the earth and not the abandonment of it. These emerging Presence driven leaders find their citizenship in heaven (Philippians 3:20). Heaven is not just where they are going, but where they have come from. They are not wanting to make heaven their home, but make their home like heaven. The time has come to raise up Presence driven leaders to inflict damage on the powers of darkness and superimpose the Kingdom of God. We have coexisted with darkness way too long. These Presence driven leaders will put a new face on the 21st Century church. They will move beyond the days of revival and usher in a Kingdom reformation that will prepare the way for the return of Christ.

During the church age, there has not been a move of God that has sustained the Presence of God for the next generation. History has revealed they have only lasted a few years. The day has dawned when Presence driven leaders will lead their generation into a greater glory. One of the greatest revivals in church history was the Welsh revival that took place a little over 100 years ago. For the very short period of time it lasted, it was one of the greatest moves of God the church has ever witnessed. This revival touched a whole nation. Evangelically speaking, they won a nation for Jesus, but they did not transform it and occupy it.

Therefore, 100 years later the spiritual landscape has not changed in Wales. It has actually become worse. Less than 3% of the Welsh population claims to be Christian today. Many souls were won in the Welsh revival, but they fell short of the glory by not making disciples. Discipling Presence driven leaders is imperative as we prepare for the coming moves of the Spirit. These Presence driven leaders will not only usher in the greatest revival in church history, but they will establish the Kingdom of God upon the earth sustaining His Presence for generations to come. The only thing that will sustain a move of God from one generation to the next is raising up mature disciples to carry the torch of God's Presence to the next generation.

During the last 2,000 years the church has experienced visitation from the Lord, but now we have moved into a paradigm shift in which Presence driven leaders will bring the habitation of God's presence into the whole earth.

> **The only thing that will sustain a move of God from one generation to the next is raising up mature disciples to carry the torch of God's Presence to the next generation**

But as truly as I live all the earth shall be filled with the glory of the Lord.

NUMBERS 14:21

As Presence driven leaders we must occupy until He comes (Luke 19:13). One of the definitions of "to occupy" is "to invest." We must invest and pour into the next generation what God has invested in us. Presence driven leaders carry an anointing upon their life that is meant to be given away. The purpose of power is to empower others!

Elijah emptied himself and invested into Elisha, his follower. Elijah went to heaven broke, he gave all that he had away. Success has nothing to do with the accumulation of wealth, our popularity, books we have written, or the status of our business. Success is measured by the degree of anointing you pour out to the next generation. That's real success!

Jesus told his disciples that our fruit should be passed to the next generation (John 15:16). Elijah was totally spent when he left the planet. He went to heaven totally bankrupt, pouring out his anointing, gifting, ability, and passion. I personally want to leave this world empty—giving away my love, joy, passion, gifts, heart, ability, wisdom, and anointing. The emerging Presence driven leaders spend their lives giving their life away. You will never truly know what is in you until you find the place to pour it out. Jesus said that He did not come to be ministered to, but to minister to others.

The anointing upon a Presence driven leader's life is for service. Anointings never leave the planet. Elijah went up to heaven, but his mantle came down upon Elisha. In Acts 1, Jesus ascended up to heaven but in Acts 2, His Holy Ghost mantle came down upon

120 Presence driven people. Heaven does not need your anointing. Heaven is doing really good without it—there is no sickness, death, or sorrow there. Your anointing is desperately needed in the earth.

This whole new breed of Presence driven leaders are about to change the present landscape of our society. They will learn to pass the torch of God's Presence from one generation to the next. We must arise as Presence driven leaders to prepare our generation to change the world. We must now redefine the future and then reshape it by bringing a Kingdom culture to our generation.

This new breed of leadership is not tyrannical leadership, but servant leadership. The greatest leaders in the coming move of the Spirit will be those who serve the people they lead. These leaders recognize and honor greatness when they see it. They will esteem others higher than themselves and honor others with the gifts and anointings they have. It is time to turn followers into leaders and leaders into world changers.

> **The greatest leaders in the coming move of the Spirit will be those who serve the people they lead**

These emerging echelon leaders are moving from a "me" to a "we" who will bring strategies together that will establish the Kingdom of God in the earth. Their lives are birthed around Kingdom cause. Their leadership acumen is of the highest order. They are selfless, having no jealousy for their comrades, nor do they jostle for recognition or position, nor will they joust those they are following or those who are following them. They never compete with one another, only complete one another. Mere civilians do not understand their commitment around their cause. Only these Presence driven leaders understand the high call of God upon their lives and their followers' lives. This next move is not about getting the city into the church, but about getting the church into the city. We must now create a global leadership perspective, empowering leaders for societal change.

This book is filled with about 700 quotes that I pray will be a clarion call to awaken the Presence driven leader in you and the purpose and plan of God in your life. May this be a handbook to inspire you, equip you, and prepare you to be part of this new breed of world changing leadership—the Presence driven leader.

—DR. MARK KAUFFMAN
September, 2017

"The **PURPOSE** of **POWER** is to **POUR** it **OUT**."

Chapter One

The Presence Driven Leader

The Lord extends a special grace to those who are committed to His Presence. David was such a person, known as a man after God's own heart. Stated more clearly, David was a man after God. He did not pursue wealth, power, a throne, or a position—he was in hot pursuit after God. In the book of Revelation, the church of Philadelphia received the Key of David. I believe this key is the Presence driven life.

One of the most notable contrasts between Saul and David is that Saul was position driven when David was Presence driven. Saul did everything in his power to keep his position while David did everything in his power to keep the Presence of God in his life. When Samuel was sent to the house of Jesse to anoint a new king, he bypassed Jesse's seven elder sons until he found a Presence driven boy by the name of David. David's resume was quite different than his brothers. As a Presence driven worshipper, he was being groomed and prepared to become a Presence driven leader. As Samuel did when he went to the house of Jesse, the Spirit of God is looking to and fro in the earth today to anoint a company of Presence driven leaders that He can commission as kings and priests and world changers. These Presence driven leaders will receive the Key of David—a key which denotes authority and can open doors that no man can shut and shut doors that no man can open (Revelation 3:7).

Just as David was promoted to be a Presence driven leader, so will the Holy Spirit promote and elevate a company of Presence driven leaders to rule at the top of their spheres. This army of leaders will be granted such great authority in the coming days that they will be given the keys to their cities, closing gates of disease and poverty. Drug cartels will be locked out of their cities, unable to pedal their drugs. Racism and every form of prejudice will no longer be welcome in their cities. These Presence driven leaders will shift atmospheres, making it impossible for such wicked principalities and powers to operate inside the cities where they walk in authority.

The Lord is raising up and promoting a Presence driven generation

The Lord is raising up and promoting a Presence driven generation. Promotion will not come to the skilled, talented, or educated, but to the Presence driven person. The American church has become more purpose driven than they are Presence driven. I believe in a purpose driven life, but I question if we have put the cart before the horse. I believe our emphasis should first and foremost be on the Presence of the Most High. Many purpose driven mentalities have become idols in the church, forgetting that our true purpose in the Kingdom of God is to be intimate with the Father, and neglecting our true destiny—to reveal Him to our generation (Psalm 71:18). God's Presence must become our priority.

> *And he said unto them, How is it that ye sought me? Wist ye not that I must be about my Father's business?*

LUKE 2:49

When at the age of twelve, Jesus modeled true intimacy with these words: "I must be about my Father." As it appears in scripture, the word business in this verse is presented in italics, and is not included in the original translation. Presence driven leaders must be about their Father.

> *To redeem them that were under the law, that we might receive the adoption of sons. And because ye are sons, God hath sent forth the Spirit of his Son into your hearts, crying, "Abba, Father."*

GALATIANS 4:5-6

The blood of Jesus Christ first purchased us and placed us into sonship, then poured the Spirit of the Son into our hearts so we can manifest the Father to our generation. The passion of the Holy Spirit is birthed within every Spirit-filled believer to have a Presence driven life. An earmark of an echelon leader is to live a Presence driven life!

Presence is Greater than Purpose

I know thy works, and thy labour, and thy patience, and how thou canst not bear them which are evil: and thou hast tried them which say they are apostles, and are not, and hast found them liars: And hast borne, and hast patience, and for my name's sake hast laboured, and hast not fainted. Nevertheless **I have somewhat against thee, because thou hast left thy first love**. *Remember therefore from whence thou art fallen, and repent, and do the first works; or else I will come unto thee quickly, and will remove thy candlestick out of his place, except thou repent.*

REVELATIONS 2:2-5 (Emphasis Added)

In this scripture, Jesus commended the church at Ephesus for her great works (purpose driven), but then she received a great rebuke because she lost her first love (Presence driven). Everything in Christ's Kingdom must have balance.

Mary and Martha lived in the same house. Mary was Presence driven while Martha was purpose driven. Jesus commended Mary for choosing the better part. The scriptures did not say Martha was wrong, only that Mary's part was better. We definitely need Martha in the house (purpose driven life), but we need a whole lot more of Mary in the house (Presence driven life). Mary and Martha's brother Lazarus received an extravagant miracle. When Jesus showed up at the graveyard of Lazarus, Martha came to Jesus and said, "Lord if you would have been here my brother would not have died." Jesus responded to Mary's [*Martha*] statement by giving her a great teaching:

> *Jesus said unto her, "I am the resurrection, and the life: he that believeth in me, though he were dead, yet shall he live: And whosoever liveth and believeth in me shall never die. Believest thou this?"*

JOHN 11:25-26

Scripture tells us that immediately after, Mary came to Jesus and seeing Him, fell at His feet in a posture of worship. Martha received a good teaching, but Mary (who was Presence driven) received her brother back from the dead. When Jesus raised him from the dead, this extravagant miracle was a direct result of Mary's extravagant Presence driven life. A Presence driven leader will host a parade of miracles that will lead this generation into the glory of God. Only those who become possessed by His Presence will be ready to possess the promises of God. The early church was known as the people of His Presence. Once again, the Lord is raising up a company of uncommon leaders who will be known for their Presence driven life. A new day has dawned in which gifting and ability pale in the presence of a Presence driven leader.

Only those who become possessed by His Presence will be ready to possess the promises of God

Moses was so Presence driven, that immediately after the Exodus out of Egypt, he led three million people back to Mt. Sinai, the place where he first encountered the Presence of God. Presence driven leaders are always anxious to lead their followers into fresh encounters with His Presence. The new breed of leaders emerging today will lead their followers into greater encounters with the Lord than what they themselves have experienced. Moses longed for the children of Israel to see this burning bush. But upon his return he led them into a much greater encounter than what he had experienced—the whole mountain was on fire—not just a burning bush. My prayer is that God would raise you up as a Presence driven leader who will lead your followers into greater encounters with the Lord than what you have experienced in days gone by.

> *Now there was long war between the house of Saul and the house of David: but David waxed stronger and stronger, and the house of Saul waxed weaker and weaker.*
>
> 2 SAMUEL 3:1

In 1984 I was employed as a designer in the second oldest flower shop in America. Within the company there were more qualified and skilled designers than me. I saw little room for advancement as there were several partners with ownership in the company. After seeking the Lord concerning my future there, the Lord spoke to me and said: "I did not place you here to take you out, but to take over," so I committed myself to a Presence driven life. As a result, the Lord anointed me to outgrow my personal limitations. Over the course of a few years, I overcame the giant opposition within the ranks of the company. I am now the CEO of that company and have transitioned it into a Kingdom business. I am living proof that the Presence driven life will wax you stronger and stronger until you prevail in every aspect of life. The passion that the Lord has given me to write this book is to see the readers be raised up as a company of Presence driven leaders who will rule over all their enemies, just like David.

Author's Note

At the conclusion of each chapter you will find a series of quotes which relate to a different aspect of the life of a Presence driven leader. These quotes have become part of me. Many have undoubtedly been placed in my spirit through pastors, mentors, and leaders from whom I have learned much. My entire life is a composite of what I have read and heard from both God and men. I have taken it all in and made these truths my own. In no way do I wish to claim credit for ideas which may have originated from others, but these quotes are now so much a part of my fabric, I honestly cannot single out which thread in the tapestry came from who. Know that I give honor to all those who have gone before me, all who have invested in my life, and all who wisely stewarded the revelation God gave to them and diligently passed to me. I trust the quotes will both motivate and inspire you as they help crystalize the truths they represent.

Quotes For a Presence Driven Leader

"Find your joy in Jesus not your calling. Your calling will disappoint you, Jesus never will."

"Are you up to date with being filled with the Holy Ghost?"

"And be not drunk with wine, wherein is excess; but be filled with the Spirit …" (Ephesians 5:18).

"You have two lives: your outer life is your reputation with mankind, your inner life is your relationship with the Lord. He looks upon your heart."

 "As a Presence driven leader, your first appointment every day should be with Jesus."

"A Presence driven leader's real stamp of approval is God's Presence on his life."

"Presence driven leaders are established in the Word of God, not the accolades of mere men."

 "Every blessing is for the Master's use, that is a leader's mentality."

"Leaders are never swayed by personalities or opinions; they are only governed by 'thus saith the Lord!'"

"The most dangerous thing for a leader is to know what God is doing and not do it. To him this is sin."

"Leaders are not governed by outside inspiration, but by inside revelation."

"What stands against you is small compared to the One who stands in you."

"Once you see yourself as God sees you, you won't need all those crazy people in your life."

"What's insanity? Making decisions apart from the Lord."

"Presence driven leaders have great hate and great love, they love what God loves and hate what God hates."

"Thou hast loved righteousness, and hated iniquity; therefore God, even thy God, hath anointed thee with the oil of gladness above thy fellows" (Hebrews 1:9).

"The greatest compliment the Lord can give you is to say, "I have need of you!""

"God invested way too much in you to leave you in that mess."

"Give yourself to the Lord like you gave yourself to sin."

"Here is the punch line: the ultimate plan of God is to reveal Himself in and through you to your generation."

"But when it pleased God, who separated me from my mother's womb, and called me by his grace, To reveal his Son in me, that I might preach him among the heathen; immediately I conferred not with flesh and blood" (Galatians 1:15-16).

"Anything that keeps you from God, run from it. Anything that leads you to God, run after it."

"I have failed and I have succeeded, neither define me—God's grace defines me."

"Always find your true identity in Christ, not your vocation, your ministry, or in success."

"Grace enables you to handle the pain of waiting."

"Your secret life with God prepares you for your public life with people."

"If you love God you will hate sin, if you love sin, you will quench your love for God."

"Salvation will save people, the Holy Ghost will fill people, and the Kingdom will change people."

"How can you not do great things when greatness is within you?"

"When a man pursues God's Presence and purpose, he moves in a gathering anointing, picking up everything pertaining to his call."

"Don't be swayed by personalities or programs, but only with His Presence."

"The absence of His Presence makes your power inoperative. Create a Presence driven life!"

"It's awesome to know what we <u>have</u> in Christ, but it's much greater to know who we <u>are</u> in Christ."

"Christ is not to be added to your life, He must become your life."

"Man can fake worship, but cannot fake being a worshipper. This is what the Father seeks."

"But the hour cometh, and now is, when the true worshippers shall worship the Father in spirit and in truth: for the Father seeketh such to worship Him" (John 4:23).

"Don't meet Jesus just once, keep meeting Him!"

"When I know the I AM, then I'll know who I am."

"The fear of the Lord will cause you to run to God and run from sin."

"The fear of the Lord is a holy awe and reverence for God, for His will, and for His ways so much that it neglects everything that offends Him."

"The one who is able to accept darkness, flatness, hardship, and rejection with joy is the one who truly lives for the Lord."

"Never define God by your experiences, but by His Word."

"Don't let people decide for you, let the Word of the Lord decide for you."

"The closer I move toward the Lord, the farther I move away from evil—that's HOLINESS."

"Presence driven leaders know wisdom is greater than weapons of war."

"Presence driven leaders obey God's commands over man's demands."

"Presence driven leaders don't look for the move of God, they are the move of God."

"Leaders are not governed by appearances and emotions, but by principles and patterns."

"Leaders live life with no regrets so one day they will hear, "Well done.'"

"Presence driven leaders with inspiration move into perspiration."

"Every Presence driven leader has a voice filled with God's heart."

"Presence driven leaders always lead their followers into divine encounters."

"God will only give you the Presence you are willing to guard."

"God has no needs only desires, but if we fulfill His desires we will have no needs."

"Fear of man is your greatest bondage, and the fear of God is your greatest freedom."

"Don't get so caught up in your situation that you miss your revelation."

"The worst place to be is where God was."

"God saved you so He could replace you with Himself: Replacement Theology 101."

"The Holy Ghost is an arsonist, He wants to set you on fire."

"When the Lord puts His hand on you, it doesn't mean He is coming to bless you, but to take possession of the vessel you are."

"When a man is possessed by His Presence, he is ready for His promises."

"Avoid things that quench your love for Jesus."

"True power in this life is not found in how much we possess in God, but by how much He possesses us."

"Presence driven leaders follow the pattern of Jesus who was more anointed than He was famous."

"Your salvation should affect your lives, home, marriage, job, bodies, and finances."

"Your prayer, praise, pursuit, persistence ,and passion escort suddenlies into your life."

"Most people see your earthen vessel, but never see the treasure within (2 Corinthians 4:7)."

"Don't brag on what you know, brag on who you know. Make your God big!"

"The Lord's love for you is relentless. He will not rest until everything hurting you is under your feet."

"The LORD said unto my Lord, Sit thou at my right hand, until I make thine enemies thy footstool" (Psalms 110:1).

"Those who know their God shall do great exploits.
Intimacy with the Lord comes before great exploits."

"Love must be expressed: God so loved the world
He gave! Loving and giving are synonymous."

"If you're not prepared for change, you're not prepared for God!"

"Prayer is not changing the mind of God, it's getting the mind of God"

"If you're not living the life you were created
to live, people won't see God in you!"

"Don't let life's circumstances dictate who God is in your life."

"Natural men are led by external inspiration, while
spiritual men are moved by internal revelation."

**"For as many as are led by the Spirit of God,
they are the sons of God." Romans 8:14**

"Stay focused on WHO blesses you,
instead of HOW He blesses you."

"If you make God big, your problems will be small. Make Him big and watch your problems shrink. O magnify the Lord!"

"The greatest way to silence your enemies
is THE JOY OF THE LORD!"

"Do you want more of the Lord? If you move <u>to</u> Him, you'll be moved <u>by</u> Him, and then you can move <u>for</u> Him!"

"Draw nigh to God, and he will draw nigh to you. Cleanse your hands, ye sinners; and purify your hearts, ye double minded" (James 4:8).

"Presence driven leaders know without Him they can do nothing."

"Grace does not excuse your hang-ups, it empowers you to hang-up your hang-ups."

"How God defines you is all that matters, not someone's crazy opinion of you."

"If it's my thing then it's nothing, it must be a God thing."

"Grace is God's ability to help you keep it together when you're going through hell."

"People always want His blessings on their terms, when His blessings follow His procedures and protocol."

"Proof of your desire is your passionate pursuit. Start your Presence driven life today."

"Learn to live in time while being loyal to eternity."

"Your work is an expression of your worship unto the Lord."

"PRESENCE DRIVEN leaders do whatever **EXCITES** the Lord!"

Chapter Two

Leading In Crisis

The greatness of leadership never emerges out of good times, but through bad times. Anyone can lead in comfort. Anyone can lead in prosperous and healthy climates, but real leaders emerge out of a crisis. Throughout history, great leaders were defined during critical times.

- President Ronald Reagan: his leadership led to the collapse of the Soviet Union.

- Sir Winston Churchill: emerged as the greatest war time leader of the 20th Century. He also won the Nobel Peace Prize and was the first person awarded an honorary citizenship in the United States.

- Abraham Lincoln: as the 16th president of the United States, he led us through a Civil War. His leadership preserved the Union, abolished slavery, and strengthened our nation through crisis. President Lincoln stood for his biblical convictions and led America into peace. ✶

- David: his leadership wasn't revealed until Saul's army was challenged by Goliath and the Philistine armies.

- Esther: came to the kingdom in the time of crisis and saved her people.

- Joseph: emerged as a dynamic leader in a time of famine. Great leadership emerges in the midst of crisis.

Frustration is common among leaders who are waiting their turn. Churchill's call to lead was delayed until crisis showed up. Abraham Lincoln's leadership was delayed until all hell broke loose in the nation. David remained in obscurity until a giant showed up, and Joseph remained in a penal institution until famine struck the land.

✗ **Frustration is common among leaders who are waiting their turn**

Many reading this book right now are experiencing frustration in your life while waiting your turn. Remember, in the days of Esther every maid had their turn—your turn will come when the right crisis shows up!

✶ Crisis does not change leaders for the worse, but for the better. Note David's response:

Thou preparest a table before me in the presence of mine enemies: thou anointest my head with oil; my cup runneth over.

PSALM 23:5 (KJV)

The crisis came to make David look good. Crisis announces that something is about to be birthed. Much like a pregnant woman in birthing pains, these pains are announcing that something is about to be born.

Crises are the hinges of the door of opportunity. In the verse below, the Apostle Paul saw his adversaries as a great door of opportunity:

For a great door and effectual is opened unto me, and there are many adversaries.

1 CORINTHIANS 16:9

Crisis and uncomfortable environments are the catalysts for creativity. Crisis brings discovery of what's inside of you and brings it to the surface. You can shake a grape, talk to a grape, but only pressure releases what is inside the grape. Crisis unveils the innate gifts of God within you and brings them to the surface.

During the Great Depression and into the 1940s, several billionaire families created more wealth in that time than any other time in the history of America. The reason was because they solved a problem in a time of crisis. Opportunity hides in crisis, wealth hides in crisis, and favor hides itself in crisis.

If you are going through a personal crisis you are probably in a season of preparation in which God is teaching you how to manage and steward the chaos. Like David, you must overcome your lion and bear in private as part of the process to prepare you to take out giants in public. Never forget in times of crisis that crisis comes to make you look good. Anyone can lead in comfort, but uncomfortable environments are the catalyst for creativity.

Never forget there is always purpose for the crisis, much like David who faced Goliath who said, "Is there not a cause?" There is always a purpose for the crisis. Crisis on the outside releases the conqueror on the inside. Crisis comes to bring the conqueror out of you!

I pray that the quotes on crisis in this chapter will empower you to lead in the coming days of crisis.

Quotes for Leading In Crisis

"Opportunities hide themselves in crisis."

"Your seed is your key to get out of crisis."

"When crisis comes it only comes to make you look good."

"Every creative miracle flows out of a crazy crisis."

"Great leaders are born in chaos not in comfort."

"Comfort is the enemy of creativity."

"Brokenness prepares you for usefulness."

"Chaos is the breeding ground of creativity."

"Chaos has the properties to bring the conqueror out of you!"

"Pressure comes to make you look good."

"God never, never, never wastes pain: pain always come with a purpose."

"Your pain has great redemptive value and purpose."

"Comfort makes you sleepy. Crisis makes you seek. Suddenlies come to seekers not sleepers."

"Crisis leads to offensive strategies."

"Great opportunities come out of crisis."

"When facing crisis, rehearse the memories that give you hope. When David faced Goliath he remembered the lion and the bear."

"Your place of pain is your opportunity to reign."

"The assignment against you is a sign of what you're assigned to rule."

"Crushings are the evidence you're called."

"If there is an entrance to trouble there will be an exit also. Prepare your exit strategy!"

"Need and lack are the mother of all miracles."

"Presence driven leaders are always delivered into situations that only God can deliver them out of."

"Crisis does not have the power to determine your end result. You do!"

"A diamond is but a piece of charcoal that went through a stressful season."

"The only battles you'll lose are the ones you don't engage in."

"You'll never know who your companions are until you have tribulation."

"I John, who also am your brother, and companion in tribulation, and in the kingdom and patience of Jesus Christ ..." (Revelation 1:9a).

"Chaos is the atmosphere for the door of opportunity."

"For a great door and effectual is opened unto me, and there are many adversaries" (1 Corinthians 16:9).

"Uncomfortable environments are the catalyst to creativity."

"Great leadership is not measured in good times, but in times of crisis."

"You never go out of your circumstances, you grow out of them."

"Pressure is a sign of a birthing season in your life."

"Wounds from a friend are better than kisses
from your enemy … beware of kiss-ups!"

"The more crisis you go through the more dangerous you are."

"Take authority over what opposes you by releasing
the opposite. We overcome evil with good."

"Crisis announces something is about to happen for your good."

"Let crisis lead you into offensive strategies."

"Adversity is the doorway into your kingdom storehouse."

"Leaders never let circumstances determine
who God is in their life."

"You're only as strong as your ability to stand in the midst of crisis."

"Divine desperation precedes NEW BEGINNINGS."

"Those who lead in crisis refuse to give their circumstances energy."

"Presence driven leaders never grow a wishbone
where a backbone ought to be."

"Leaders in crisis never flirt with indecision."

"Leaders born in crisis know that if it was
easy everyone could do it."

"If you are in
CRISIS then you're
a **CANDIDATE** for
MIRACLES."

Chapter Three

The Communication of a Leader

A s Presence driven leaders, we are called to be co-creators with Christ. We are to speak and create out of the Kingdom of God which is righteousness, peace, and joy in the Holy Ghost. Releasing the Kingdom creates the environment necessary to function as a Son of God and as a Presence driven leader.

Our mind is a blueprint of what we desire to build in the natural realm, but our mouth is the birth canal that gives our thoughts life and existence. As a Presence driven leader, we are to be in charge of our present realities by taking responsibility of our thoughts and words, co-creating with the Lord daily.

Sound ushers in every new movement of the Spirit of God. Sound is an integral part of God's Kingdom culture. It is imperative to understand that nothing leaves heaven until someone speaks from heaven. The new breed of leaders God is raising up in this present hour make corresponding sounds with heaven. Nothing happens in the earth until someone makes corresponding sounds. Every leader is called to communicate what is being said in the heavens upon the earth.

> *Thy Kingdom come, Thy will be done in earth, as it is in heaven.*
>
> MATTHEW 6:10

The truth of the matter is we are to hear what heaven is saying and then repeat it in the earth. Elijah was a Presence driven leader who had heard the sound of abundance in the heavens and prophetically communicated that sound within the earth! By communicating the right sound in the earth, that sound became his reality. He said, "I hear the sound of the abundance …" and the result was an abundance of rain. Once again, nothing happens in the earth until someone makes corresponding sounds on earth in agreement with heaven.

Presence driven leaders communicate the right sounds in the earth that will ensure the next move of God in your life. Every leader must learn how to communicate the right sound that will flow out of their teaching, serving, giving, character, vision, life, and vocabulary. Every leader must guard and preserve the sound; for the sound of the leader communicates the vision and governs the dynamics of his follower's destiny.

We have too many people communicating the wrong sounds in the earth, therefore communicating the wrong message. Elijah declared it was going to rain long before there was evidence of rain. The Presence driven leader declares prophetic things over their followers while others are declaring drought, recession, and lack. Such leaders are risk takers declaring prosperity, blessing, and favor upon their followers and everyone under their care.

When you communicate something, your life must back your words. As a leader, teaching is best done when information meets demonstration. What you say as a leader will be empowered by who you are.

The truth of the matter is that words are not always necessary to communicate to the people within our sphere. This new breed of leader in the 21st Century is going to move beyond the excellence of words into the excellence of Presence.

Remember the four lepers in the days of Elisha? They defeated their enemies, broke famine, plundered the enemies' tents … and did it all without words. This next move of God is bigger than words. This Presence driven leadership carries the Presence of God so strongly that even their shadows will heal people and transform lives. Remember the story of Simon Peter? While walking down the street he healed the sick and delivered those with unclean spirits by just overshadowing them with the Presence he carried—he did it without words. This is much like the woman with the alabaster box who anointed the head and feet of Jesus and filled the atmosphere with fragrant oil. So powerful was the Presence she carried, it rebuked and restrained her enemies without words. There is no mention in scripture of Benjamin ever speaking a word,

This next move of God is bigger than words

but everything happened when he showed up: famine ended, his brothers were reconciled, and family inheritances were released … all without him saying even one word.

We are thankful for the excellence of words within great leaders of the days gone by, but in the coming moves of the Spirit, words may not be necessary. The excellence of God's Presence upon a leader will communicate what heaven is saying to this generation.

Quotes for The Communication of a Leader

"Communication is the basis of relationship."

"There is no progress without healthy communication."

"If we don't communicate we will never relate."

"Communication eliminates confusion, misunderstanding, and offenses."

"You can cancel all negative words with words of life."

"Rise up and start speaking as a son of God and not as a desperate sinner."

"Listening is the art of communication."

"Success is found not in your ability to speak, but to listen."

"Maintaining harmony between leaders and followers takes work."

"The most energy demanding duty a leader
can engage in is communication."

"All covenant relationships require communication."

"To be silent is not being safe."

"Uncommon leaders speak to your potential,
knowing it will produce your potential."

"What you talk about, you will bring about."

**"Death and life are in the power of the tongue: and they
that love it shall eat the fruit thereof" (Proverbs 18:21).**

"The loudest voices shape the culture."

"Presence driven leaders voice the naked truth and don't dress it up."

"This is the hour for Presence driven leaders
to speak up and speak out."

"Let your words and actions create an environment
that others want to be a part of."

"Your words, your thoughts, and your prayers
are writing the next chapter of your life."

"Like the prophet Elijah call forth your next season.
Declare, 'I hear the sound of abundance!'"

"Uncommon leaders speak to your potential not your problem."

"Your **WORD**
is the **FINAL
AUTHORITY** in
your world. **GUARD**
your words."

Chapter Four

A Leader's Destiny

Simply stated, our purpose is to be intimate with the Lord, and our destiny is to manifest Him. Our true fulfillment is found in God's Presence. Our destiny and provision are found in the place of His Presence—all resulting from a Presence driven life. This book was written for leaders to upgrade their intimacy and encounter the Lord so they may be a part of the emerging Presence driven leadership.

Motion is essential to fulfill your destiny. A car must be in gear and in motion to get to its destination. You can't even turn without motion. Who cares what kind of car you have as long as it moves? God creates different vehicles which are created to take you into your journey and destiny. The vehicle He uses may change from time to time. In one season you may feel like you are in a jalopy and the next season you might feel like you are in a Porsche. As long as you are in motion, you can make it to your destination.

Purpose is heaven's will for your life, but destiny is when your will and heaven's purpose merge and this is walked out on the earth. Destiny walks out purpose. Destiny and destination are not the same thing. Destination is

Destiny walks out purpose

reached when you finish and fulfill your destiny. Destiny is a journey. Purpose comes in theory, but destiny makes it practical. When you begin to walk out destiny, you create your own momentum and movement. The purpose is decided by God, destiny is decided by human choice. When you are fulfilling your destiny, you come alive.

The strong impression of the dreams you are having right now is your future visiting you. As you move towards your destiny, your destiny moves towards you. Never do desperate things, only do destiny things. There must be a "no excuse" policy when fulfilling your destiny. Behind every excuse is just a lack of desire.

Where you have been does not determine where you are going. Your past and present do not define you, your destiny does. A clear revelation of your destiny will keep you alive in the face of contradiction. Embrace your destiny and you will find your future is waiting for you, prepared for you, and has need of you.

When your destiny converges with God's set time you will collide with power, provision, and a fresh encounter with God's Presence. God is doing something so crazy in your future that you can feel it

[handwritten margin note: we manifest Him when walking intimately w/ Him]

in the present. Never forget that times don't create the people, people create the times. As you move and fulfill your destiny, you will create a momentous movement that cannot be stopped. Dare to believe big and your destiny will unfold!

Never be discouraged while you are in the process of fulfilling your destiny. You must fall in love with the process if you want to enter into greatness. Never underestimate the destiny God has for you.

> *Now unto him that is able to do exceeding abundantly above all that we ask or think, according to the power that worketh in us …*

EPHESIANS 3:20

You are empowered to do more than you expect. There is a measure of power operative in you right now to do more than you think you can. The potential for greatness resides within you; therefore, the greatness of your destiny in your future resides within you right now. There is more to you than what meets the eye. Your destiny isn't by chance, but it is a designed destiny God has planned for you.

> *For I know the thoughts that I think toward you, saith the Lord, thoughts of peace, and not of evil, to give you an expected end.*

JEREMIAH 29:11

No one can fulfill your destiny but you; therefore, be authentic and be real. No one can do it like you, say it like you, or express it like you. Quit living someone else's dream. Stop chasing someone else's destiny and start living the designed destiny God has purposed for you.

[handwritten: UAS!]

It is God's designed destiny for you that defines you, not some crazy person's opinion of you or your circumstances. God never blesses immobility. Rise up today and begin moving towards your destiny and watch your destiny move towards you.

Quotes For a Leader's Destiny

"The proof of your desire is in your pursuit."

"To the persevering leader there is always an expiration date on trouble."

"Dissatisfaction is the progenitor of change."

"You'll have to fall in love with the process if you're going to enter into greatness."

"I want to look more like where I'm going than where I've been."

"Risk releases leaders into the realm of possibilities."

"Leaders seize the moment or miss their season."

"Great leaders are not born in ivory palaces, but in the wilderness."

"Real leaders don't have large followings, they go where most are not willing to go."

"Leaders never do desperate things, they do destiny things."

"The potential for greatness resides within you."

"Your calling and assignment is never predicated on your past or your present, but upon God's promises."

"How God defines you determines your life, not man's opinion."

"Uncommon leaders love everybody, but do not work with everybody."

"The future belongs to those who prepare for it."

"Frustration with your present creates your future."

"It doesn't matter where you have been, it only matters where you are going."

"You have been summoned by the Lord to change the course of history."

"God never created anything with the thought in mind that it was going to fail."

"Start policing your world and tell bad things, 'TIME IS UP!'"

"Your limitations have absolutely nothing to do with your expectations."

"Salvation gets you the next life, the Kingdom releases that life NOW!"

"You'll never change your future until you change your present."

"Your mistakes are never as big as your destiny."

"Your destiny is locked up in your seed. START SOWING!"

"The most dangerous thing about you is that you are still alive after all the hell you've endured."

"An echelon leader's darkest hour will become his finest moment."

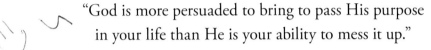

"God is more persuaded to bring to pass His purpose in your life than He is your ability to mess it up."

"Your destiny is bigger than your mess."

"You are wired to WIN!"

"When you pray out of your future, you pray out your future."

"You cannot run away from who you are! Your destiny chases you."

"When a man is dissatisfied where he is it is because he visited his future. You are more suited for your future than your present."

"Your enemy does not attack you because of where you are, but because of where you are going."

"Your individual destiny is found in your corporate identity."

"Leaders recognize that siftings precede shiftings."

"Your mistakes are not as big as your destiny."

"Your closest friends and family will not see your calling."

"Don't struggle to be who you're not called to be, labor only to enter into what you were born to be."

"Choose an occupation you love and you'll never work another day in your life."

"If it's impossible for God to make a mistake,
how can anyone be a mistake?"

"Risk is the evidence that you believe."

"Quit living someone else's lie about you, live
the truth of what God says about you."

"The potential for greatness resides within you."

"Leaders find their identity in God, not in their profession."

"When God is ready to shift your season, He brings a need."

"What is ahead of you is greater than what is behind you."

"Your seed has a right to live."

"Don't anchor crazy people in your life. Cut
them loose so your ship can move."

"Real leaders want to look more like where they are going than where they have been."

"One man says, 'I can't,' another man says, 'I
can,' both are right. Choose well!"

**"I can do all things through Christ which strengtheneth me.
Your calling and assignment was God's idea" (Philippians 4:1).**

"Frustration with your present carves a pathway into your future."

"God doesn't reward you by how you start, but by how you finish."

"If God started something in you, it's a sign He will finish it!"

"Being confident of this very thing, that he which hath begun a good work in you will perform it until the day of Jesus Christ" (Philippians 1:6).

 "God is after the recovery of the earth, not to have you abandon it."

"You're good enough to be what you were born to do."

"The fight you're in reveals that you are chosen for greatness."

 "Many are called, but few choose the Presence driven life."

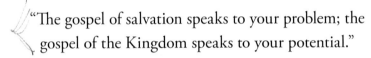 "The gospel of salvation speaks to your problem; the gospel of the Kingdom speaks to your potential."

"The wind that blows against you today will be the wind that gets behind you tomorrow—great momentum is in your future."

"No one can wear the mantle made for you! It is tailor made, one of a kind, and you wear it well!"

 "The future belongs to those who prepare for it."

 "The enemy's assignment against you is not greater than God's assignment for you."

"Your destiny is not in front of you, but resides within you."

 "What you have ahead of you is far greater than what's behind you."

 "A leader's prayers, praise, and proclamations carve out their future."

"Your calling is God's idea! Who He employs, He empowers."

"God calls you in your present what you'll be in the future."

"If God put you in the belly of your Momma,
it's a sign that He has need of you."

"Leaders prepare to do something so awesome, so huge,
and so massive, they don't have time to mess around."

"God hasn't left you, He is just moving you!
Move with the movings of God."

"What your hands have started, your hands shall finish."

**"The hands of Zerubbabel have laid the foundation of this
house; his hands shall also finish it; and thou shalt know that
the LORD of hosts hath sent me unto you" (Zechariah 4:9).**

"Quit running with donkeys when you're a
horse. Please get in the right race!"

"Leaders would much rather wear out than rust out."

"When you feel like throwing in the towel, it's just
before your breakthrough. Hold onto that towel!
There will be NO towel throwing in this race."

**"We learn from the past to do in the
present what will provide in the future."**

"Leaders refuse to let anything deter them from finishing."

"The Lord rewards finishers."

"The Lord never starts anything with the intention of failing! If you fail it's your choice."

"Just before your suddenly will be silence."

"Just before a suddenly, your circumstance will scream at you."

"What seems like setbacks to you are big steps in God toward your destiny. You're closer NOW than ever!"

"For your shame ye shall have double; and for confusion they shall rejoice in their portion: therefore in their land they shall possess the double: everlasting joy shall be unto them" (Isaiah 61:7).

"Leaders show up where they need to be and not just where they want to be."

"Leaders know that greater promotions come with greater responsibility."

"Long range goals will keep you from getting frustrated with short term failures."

"The future belongs to those who prepare for it."

"A leader of destiny carries a burden to change the course of their generation."

"Destiny-minded leaders treat everyone as if they are famous."

Chapter Five

The Visionary Leader

Other than the gift of Jesus Christ, vision is your greatest gift. Vision is greater than the gift of sight because your vision governs all the processes of your life.

> *Declaring the end from the beginning, and from ancient times the things that are not yet done, saying, My counsel shall stand, and I will do all My pleasure.*

ISAIAH 46:10

Your past and present do not define you, but your vision does. We must view everything through the eyes of vision. The poorest man on the planet is not the man without money, but a man without vision. Vision is an incredible gift given by God.

Where there is no vision, the people perish: but he that keepeth the law, happy is he.

PROVERBS 29:18

Vision drives every decision in your life. When man is without vision he makes poor decisions. Solomon said where there is no vision people perish. Therefore, where there is vision people will prosper. People live stuck in the past because they have no vision. When men have a vision, the power of that vision will heal and deliver them from their past. I have found that people who live in past hurt, abuses, and tragedies, are normally visionless people. Vision is such a powerful force it will drive every decision you will make in your life. The greater the vision the greater decisions you will make.

> **Where there is no vision people perish ... where there is vision people will prosper**

A man with vision can take the impossible and make it possible. It is such a dynamic force that it empowers man to overcome suffering, setbacks, delays, and disappointments. Vision is the inspiration of the soul. I am thankful for the natural gift of sight, but more grateful for the spiritual gift of vision. Your vision is more powerful than your sight. Sight allows you to survey your present. Vision allows you to prophesy your future. So powerful is vision, it will anchor your vessel during the greatest storms. God gives you vision to keep you on course in times of preparation. Your vision is what brought you here to this day.

Twenty-eight years ago, the Lord gave me an open vision of my city. I saw my city as heaven saw her. I did not realize the price I would need to pay in order for this vision to be fulfilled, but that vision from twenty-eight years ago has governed my life and has been the anchor of my soul throughout the most difficult storms. It kept me alive through ten years of sickness and helped my wife and I process through six miscarriages until the Lord gave us our son, Christian Mark. It is the power of vision that causes us to overcome the most difficult circumstances in our lives.

The Lord gave the children of Israel a vision of a promised land that would flow with milk and honey. They would be given houses they would not build, wells they did not dig, and vineyards they did not plant. Then immediately following the glimpse of this promise they were driven into a dry, howling wilderness that looked nothing like the vision. A true vision from God will always lead you into contradicting circumstances, but remember that your circumstances do not determine your destiny—your vision does.

Your circumstances have not stopped the vision that is alive inside of you. Even in the greatest crucible, your vision survives. Vision is one of God's currencies and it will transition your future into the present. The most frustrated person on the planet is the person with vision. Why? Because you see the potential in your vision while living in the present. When your present does not look like your future, you experience frustration. This frustration will be the catalyst to thrust you into your future. Embrace your vision and you will find that your vision is waiting for you. Your vision has need of you.

Your vision has need of you

Never give up on your vision! When vision converges with God's set time, you will collide with power, provision, and a fresh encounter with His Presence. Vision sees God doing something so crazy in your future you can feel it in your present. Please don't allow crazy folks to block the vision of your future. You will always move in the direction of your vision—if you look down you will go down, if you look up you will go up.

Visionary people can handle the problems of the future. They sometimes have a problem handling the problems of today, but the problems of today prepare you to solve the problems in your future. Long range goals will keep you from getting frustrated with your short-term failures. True faith is God's ability to apprehend the vision of one's destiny with such a powerful grip that it cannot be taken away until it is fulfilled. True vision is knowing what God knows and seeing what God sees. When your past calls, you don't answer. Your past rarely has anything good to say, so rise up with fresh vision and say to your past, "Excuse me, I must go … my future is calling me!"

Quotes for The Visionary Leader

"Presence driven leaders see opportunity
while others see negativity."

"Faith in God includes faith in His timing."

"Visionary leaders never see where their
followers are, but where they are going."

"Presence driven leaders romanticize risk."

"Visionaries convict the visionless, they will either run from you or to you."

"Visionary leaders see crisis as the equivalent to opportunity."

"When your vision converges with your set time, you collide with power and provision."

"Your eyesight is the enemy to your vision."

"There is too much of God in you for your present world to handle, you'll need to leave leftovers when you're gone."

"To be successful in life you'll need to lose your losing mentality."

"Have you ever felt like you're an eagle among turkeys? If so, it's probably true."

"I dare you to dream big, it's the only way the world will know how big your God really is!"

"O magnify the LORD with me, and let us exalt his name together" (Psalms 34:3).

"Your vision will determine your decisions in life. The greater the vision the greater the decisions you will make every day."

"Your greatest gift after Jesus is vision."

"Thinking big will break you out of small places."

"Small minded people stay small and avoid big minded people. THINK BIG!"

"Greatness rides on the shirttail of small things."

"For who hath despised the day of small things?" (Zechariah 4:10a)

"The Kingdom of God never looks for the answer, it is the answer."

"There is a you that is greater than the you that is present."

"Ye are of God, little children, and have overcome them: because greater is he that is in you, than he that is in the world" (1 John 4:4).

"You may have a problem, but you have a promise. Your promise is the way out of your problem."

"You're waiting for a move of the Spirit? When is God never moving?"

"Every leader has a calling of creativity not comfort."

"Comfort keeps leaders locked in the realm of impossibility."

"Presence driven leaders redefine the future."

"As it is written, 'I have made thee a father of many nations,' before him whom he believed, even God, who quickeneth the dead, and calleth those things which be not as though they were" (Romans 4:17).

"Leaders never call the landscape by its present appearance, but by the seeds they sow."

"The gift of vision is greater than the gift of sight."

"The poorest man on the earth is not a man without
a dollar, but a man without a vision."

"Leaders know that God's vision is not their ambition."

"Success occurs when your dreams get bigger than your excuses."

"Great vision left unempowered is no vision at all."

Visionary leaders always build on strengths, not weaknesses."

"The ultimate goal of the Presence driven leader is
to teach their followers to serve the vision."

"The Kingdom of God doesn't need big leaders, but big thinkers."

"When you embrace your vision, you will find out your future
is waiting for you, prepared for you, and has need of you."

"Leaders preserve the vision that drives the mission."

"Yesterday we created today, today we create a better tomorrow."

"I'm more interested in having visions of
God than visions of myself."

**"Now it came to pass in the thirtieth year, in the fourth
month, in the fifth day of the month, as I was among
the captives by the river of Chebar, that the heavens
were opened, and I saw visions of God" (Ezekiel 1:1).**

"Your focus will determine your future."

"Your past and your present don't define you, your vision does."

"Vision is so powerful it governs all the processes of your life."

"Woe unto him that saith unto his father, 'What begettest thou?' or to the woman, 'What hast thou brought forth?'" (Isaiah 45:10)

"Vision is a powerful magnetic force that gravitates resources into your life."

"Vision is such a powerful force it keeps you alive."

"Never despise the small places when your vision is so big."

"The catalyst of change is your willingness to be reformed, renewed and reshaped."

"Get a vision for how much you can give away, not how much you can get"

"There is a difference with believing something and seeing something, it's called vision! What you see in your mind is what you will see manifest."

"If you can't handle the pain, you can't handle the promise."

"Every VICTORY has a war attached to it!"

"Don't praise the Lord for just what you see. Praise Him also for what you <u>want</u> to see. True faith is knowing what God knows and seeing what God sees."

"Every great vision is acquired by great faith."

"A true vision from the Lord will bring a visitation to your eyes."

"Hope (expectation) is so powerful; it releases strategies, fresh ideas, and creative formulas for success. All you need is HOPE!"

"Leaders do the most important thing every day."

"Most people build around a <u>need</u>, visionary leaders build around a <u>cause</u>."

"Have you decided to live out your moment in history? If not, begin today!"

"It's not what you want in this life, but what are you willing to do to get it."

"Your faith can do what your thinking can not."

"Great faith and great people are the results of great fights."

"There is more to you than meets the eye."

"Frustration is a friend to help you craft out a better future."

"If you think down you will go down, if you think up you will go up, as a man thinks in his heart, so is he. It's time to come up higher!"

"Our actions, hopes, dreams and attitude affect and shape generations."

"Without holiness, no man can SEE God. Therefore, without holiness we have limited VISION."

"When you focus on your **STRENGTHS**, your **WEAKNESSES** become **IRRELEVANT.**"

Chapter Six

The Preparation of a Leader

There are <u>principles</u> which must be met to succeed in moving into your next season. We are all familiar with the story of David defeating Goliath. For forty days, Israel was terrorized and paralyzed by this intimidating giant. The story tells us how Saul's army greatly feared Goliath and how Jesse sent his youngest son, David, to bring his brothers' lunch on the battlefield. David had just come out of the wilderness where he had been in a dress rehearsal for what he was about to confront. The wilderness was the place of preparation for his next season of success, promotion, and prosperity. David was prepared for the new season. He had outgrown the practice field and had now landed on the playing field.

Unless you are prepared, being at the right place at the right time will not make you successful or bring you promotion. Saul attempted to put his armor on David, but David had not proven Saul's armor. He knew he would not succeed with borrowed gifts from another leader. The sling and the stone had been proven by David in the wilderness and was all he needed on the battlefield.

Your preparation is never wasted. Missed opportunities are a direct result of an unprepared life. What you don't prepare for will never come to you. Paul says to be ready in season and out of season. Even when your gift is not needed, be ready. When prepared leaders are ready, their gifts will make room for them. You will never know when opportunity will come knocking. Success is where preparation and opportunity meet.

> **Missed opportunities are a direct result of an unprepared life**

After David's success in killing the giant, the people shouted that David slew ten thousand. In essence they said, "David, you are equal to ten thousand." A prepared life will make you equal to any problem or crucible you face. A prepared life will make you equal to the challenge. Whatever the contest or task, preparation will grant you the adequate power to succeed.

David had the solution to the crisis he would face on the battlefield. Though he wasn't skilled in the use of Saul's armor, what he had learned on the practice field—how to bring down a lion and a bear with a couple of stones and a sling—was sufficient on the playing field. He was prepared to bring down a giant with the same sling and stones. If you will quit trying to wear other people's stuff that does not fit you, you will find that what God has entrusted you with is more than sufficient. There is no one quite like you. No one can say it like you. No one can do it like you!

Become so prepared that you outgrow your limitations and outgrow your present season. You will never **go** out of your season, you will **grow** out of your season. When you are a prepared person, people will promote you, crown you, and celebrate you.

Before a manufacturer puts their products out into the marketplace, they first put them through a series of tests for quality assurance. This is done to ensure the customer is getting a quality product. So it is with the visions and dreams God has given you. Your dreams and vision must go through a series of tests. This is God's quality assurance process to ensure His product is tried, tested, and prepared. Only after passing the tests do the manufacturers put their name on the product. The same holds true in God's Kingdom.

Every leader must go through a series of testings and trials as a part of the preparatory work for their purpose. Once the preparation has been completed, they can expect manifestation of their purpose. If you are not in manifestation, you are still in preparation. If you stay in preparation, you can be assured the time will come when the Lord will usher you into days of manifestation. May the following quotes inspire you to be prepared for greatness.

Quotes for The Preparation of A Leader

"Your pain, perplexities and problems have
great redemptive value and purpose."

**"Never get weary in well doing, you are closer to your
promise than when you first believed" (Galatians 6:9).**

"When you know your purpose, you will be
equipped to handle the process."

"Your enemies put you down so God can lift you up."

"Leaders pursue their calling not their comfort. Calling is not always comfortable."

"Leaders learn to master themselves before
they try to master their world."

"Never, never, never, have an 'I wasn't ready,' moment."

"God sends the prepared leader to the common
to make the common look good."

"Are you waiting? That's just being lethargic."

"If God has designed an extraordinary plan for you, then there
will also be an extraordinary preparation for you to go through."

"You're waiting for God to move? When is God
not moving? IT'S YOUR MOVE!"

"Do the small things right and God will
promote you to big things later."

"Missed opportunities are a direct result of not being prepared."

"If you're not in your season of manifestation,
you're still in your season of preparation"

"There is nothing wrong with being wrong, but there is
something wrong with not making the right changes."

"God will let you keep trying until you get it right."

"Never forget the law of first things, your
development comes before your deliverance."

When a prepared leader touches a common
person, uncommon things happen."

"All leaders will experience rejection, but
rejection is God's protection."

"Get militant about the gifts given to you and stir them up!"

"In every new season the Lord has prepared things
for you that you are not prepared for!"

**"For since the beginning of the world men have not heard,
nor perceived by the ear, neither hath the eye seen, O
God, beside thee, what he hath prepared for him that
waiteth for him. Bring them on Jesus!" (Isaiah 64:4)**

"What is the definition of perfection? MATURITY."

"God's woundings proceed God's wonders."

"Are you having delays? When you change God hastens the process."

"Your process is designed to develop the spiritual muscles you need to sustain the weight of God's glory that resides in your future."

"God always calls leaders to do what they cannot do."

"Now unto him that is able to do exceeding abundantly above all that we ask or think, according to the power that worketh in us ..." (Ephesians 3:20).

"Everyone wants to be promoted, propelled, and prosperous without process, but process precedes promotion, propelling, and prosperity."

"You will never have a BREAKER ANOINTING if you have not been BROKEN."

Chapter Seven

The Atmosphere of a Leader

awesome

Presence driven leaders are powerful creators of atmospheres. They control environments, emotions, and energy. In creating their environments, others experience the Presence of God they carry. Through their emotions, they express the nature, love, joy, and life of their Heavenly Father. With their energy, they leave their faith, fire, power, vision, passion, and divine energy behind.

Presence driven leaders lead their followers from one degree of glory to another. Presence driven leaders never need to Google directions to lead others into the glory. It is easy to lead people to the place they live. Moses, who was a Presence driven leader, easily led three million Israelites to Mt. Sinai—the place of glory, vision, and fire—because he had been there before, he knew the way!

Uncommon leaders take dominion by taking atmospheres. The mandate for the 21st Century leader is to fill the whole earth with the glory of God. To fulfill this mandate, we must capture atmospheres. Presence driven leaders determine the atmosphere they live in. They create the measure of glory others will experience.

- What level of glory do you carry into a room?

- What atmospheres do you create when you step into the room?

- What energy do you leave behind when you depart from a room?

If your level of glory is greater than those in the room, others will submit to the greater glory of the leader who governs the atmosphere.

> *Ye are of God, little children, and have overcome them: because greater is he that is in you, than he that is in the world.*
>
> 1 JOHN 4:4

If greater is He that is in you than anything outside of you, then you will never submit to the atmosphere. The atmosphere must submit to you. Presence driven leaders master atmospheres and lead people into a divine encounter with God. What encounters will you lead people into today?

Heaven and hell both function in atmospheres. Hell cannot function in the wrong atmosphere and neither can heaven. As leaders, we take dominion over hell by controlling the atmosphere.

Presence driven leaders have mastered atmospheres by releasing days of heaven upon the earth.

> *And he put the wood in order, and cut the bullock in pieces, and laid him on the wood, and said, Fill four barrels with water, and pour it on the burnt sacrifice, and on the wood. "Do it again," he said, and they did it again. "Do it a third time," he ordered, and they did it the third time. The water ran down around the altar and even filled the trench.*
>
> 1 KINGS 18:33-35

Days of famine and drought had been in the land during the Mt. Carmel showdown between the Prophet Elijah and the prophets of Baal. Let's look at how the Prophet Elijah governed the atmosphere during the Mt. Carmel showdown. Elijah asked for twelve barrels of water to be poured on the sacrifice. Water was a rare commodity. I have often wondered where he got twelve barrels of water, because there had not been rain for three and half years. God will always ask you to give what you have need of, He will ask you to give what is precious, rare, and valuable. The very thing you need is what He will ask you to pour out. Only after he poured out the twelve barrels did God give him an open heaven and the abundance of rain was poured out.

The very thing you need is what He will ask you to pour out

Presence driven leaders pour what is needed into the atmosphere. What you pour out into the earth, the Lord will pour out from the heavens. This is one way of mastering atmospheres: release what is precious and rare and the Lord will open up the heavens and pour out in abundance. There is no good thing He will withhold when we take dominion over atmospheres by pouring out our best.

The present battle in our world is for atmospheres. We must find barren environments and impregnate them with what God has placed within us. Whatever you put in the atmosphere affects your life, your future, and all those under your care.

> *Bring ye all the tithes into the storehouse, that there may be meat in mine house, and prove me now herewith, saith the Lord of hosts, if I will not **open you** the windows of heaven, and **pour you out** a blessing, that there shall not be room enough to receive it.*
>
> MALACHI 3:10 (EMPHASIS ADDED)

I grew up being taught that as we give our tithes and offerings, God would open the windows of heaven and pour out blessings, and I believe there is an application to that teaching. But I also believe there is a greater revelation in this scripture. The Lord does not say He will open up for you the windows of heaven, but said He will open YOU the window of Heaven. He did not say He would pour out for you a blessing, but that He would pour YOU out, a blessing.

Presence driven leaders have a divine connection to the storehouse of heaven. We have a promise that God will open us up as the windows of heaven and pour us out as a blessing! Sinners are the gates of hell, while believers are the windows of heaven. Allow the Lord to open you up as a window of heaven and pour out of you the blessings that are innate within you into the atmospheres you have been given jurisdiction over.

You will never know what's in you until you find the place to give it away. This is how you release days of heaven upon the earth. The hour has come to raise up a Presence driven administration of leaders that welcome the Presence of God into the atmosphere, so others might experience His Kingdom, His power, and His glory.

Whatever approaches God must change. He is immutable, but we are mutable. Our lives are altered by His divine Presence. It is impossible to approach God without changing. So it is when others approach the Presence of God you carry. When they come in the aura of your presence something will change. Presence driven leaders have a place in God where they are so filled with Him they overflow like a cup running over. What you carry as a Presence driven leader will change atmospheres. Presence driven leaders will disrupt ungodly environments, depriving hell of its ability to function. Get ready to open up the window you are and be poured out as a blessing in the world in which you live.

Quotes for The Atmosphere of a Leader

"Create atmospheres every day that God can invade."

"You will not be rewarded for going to heaven, but for how much of heaven you give away on earth."

"Rearrange your world to look like heaven, and heaven will appear."

"Develop a prophetic environment so you can have days of heaven upon the earth."

"Our goal is not going to heaven, but bringing heaven to earth."

"It's not how much influence I have in the earth, but how much influence I have in the heavens that really matters."

"Miracles help us communicate our message."

"Thanksgiving and praise give you admission to the realm of heaven."

"Stop looking for heaven later and start looking for heaven now."

"Presence driven leaders are so intense, so desperate, and so passionate their life gets heaven's attention."

"The life of a Presence driven leader puts a demand on heaven for more."

"A Presence driven leader's reward is not heaven, but God."

"Don't make heaven your home, make your home like heaven."

"Want more heaven now? Get more Holy Ghost, He connects us with heaven."

"What makes you extremely dangerous is not your plans for heaven, but your plans to change your world."

"At the end of my life, I want the Lord to tell the angels, "This man bankrupted heaven while on earth!'"

"Do something so big for God heaven would
be embarrassed not to bring it to pass."

"The measure that you release the heavens is determined
by the measure you have experienced hell,"

"You change your earth by releasing heaven."

"The Lord's righteousness gives us access to the heavens.
The saint's righteousness releases heaven on earth."

"Learn to make sounds that correlate with heaven that will reconfigure your world. It's called the power of agreement!"

"Presence driven leaders exert great pressure
on hell to leave their territory."

"I want to invade and create atmospheres in
places that angels have never been."

"Every Presence driven leader leaves the
environment charged before they leave it."

"If I create the same atmosphere tomorrow that I have
today, I'll never have more of God in my world."

"Let your words and actions create an atmosphere
where others can encounter your God."

"Suddenlies come to atmosphere setters."

"Presence driven leaders motivate their followers
more by what they do than by what they say."

"Every **PRESENCE DRIVEN** leader leaves the environment **CHARGED** before they leave it."

Chapter Eight

The Overcoming Leader

E very great leader will have to learn the principle of overcoming. A finishing mindset is required of leaders if they are to be overcomers and finish their destiny in Christ. To be an overcomer you must be locked into finishing. An overcoming mindset is not moved by circumstances, people's opinions, setbacks, or delays. There must be nothing that deters you from finishing! God rewards finishers. It has always been, "Well done thy good and faithful servant." In the Word of God, we see that it is the overcomer who is rewarded with the promises of God.

Within every Presence driven leader there is a spirit within them driving them to a place called finish. The only way this finishing anointing is obtained is through a Presence driven life. It is not obtained through our gifts, talents, or ability—it comes through an intimate relationship with the Lord Jesus Christ. Never allow your gifts, talents, and abilities to take you where your character can't keep you. Judas had a gift for money, but he did not have the power to overcome the spirit of greed. Presence driven leaders have the power to overcome their temptations, trials, and tribulations so they can go to the next level.

Samuel mourned the death of Saul:

> *And the Lord said unto Samuel, "How long wilt thou mourn for Saul, seeing I have rejected him from reigning over Israel? Fill thine horn with oil, and go. I will send thee to Jesse the Bethlehemite: for I have provided me a king among his sons."*

1 SAMUEL 16:1

This speaks to us prophetically that we should quit mourning over the things in our life that have reigned over us and limited us from fulfilling our destiny. Everything in your past—good, bad, or ugly—can be a limitation or restraint from where the Lord wants to lead you. It is imperative that you know everything in your past has a redemptive purpose.

Everything in your past has a redemptive purpose

> *And we know that all things work together for good to them that love God, to them who are the called according to his purpose.*

ROMANS 8:28

The Lord told Samuel to fill his horn with oil and go to Jesse's house in Bethlehem where he would anoint a new king. The Lord told Samuel to get his mind off the past and get his face into the future. This finishing anointing, which is being released in the present hour, will empower you to overcome your circumstances and cause you to put your face like a flint into the future.

Once we overcome past issues we can rise, take our anointing, and participate in the new thing God is doing in the earth today. Before you anoint the new thing, you will have to receive a horn. To receive a horn, there must be a sacrifice and death. The Lord used your past to produce a death in you so He can anoint you with fresh oil and fresh purpose. Calvary came before Pentecost. Suffering precedes glory. Humility comes before exaltation, and death comes before resurrection.

A Jubilee trumpet is sounding in this hour for you to rise up, overcome, and move away from the past. Move away from your pain, perplexities, and problems and take the anointing God has created in you. Find the new thing God is doing so you can pour your oil on it. The fresh anointing the Lord is pouring out in this hour has been created by your past struggles, pains, and crucibles. It is a finishing anointing that comes only to the overcomer. Rise up today with what God has given you and take the fresh anointing poured upon your life. Prepare for the new thing God is doing in the planet.

Overcoming is the means to obtain something. Overcomers are winners who find ways to win. Losers always find a way to lose. The test for Elisha as he was following Elijah was what could stop him. In Elisha's pursuit of Elijah, Elijah seemed to discourage Elisha from following him. This test for Elisha would determine his next level of leadership. Your faith is measured by what can stop you! Yet, even with all the discouragement from Elijah, Elisha was unstoppable

Your faith is measured by what can stop you!

and locked into finishing. As a result, after Elisha's test he was rewarded with a double portion anointing. Persistence is a powerful force and those who are persistent in life win. You need to be persistent too!

In my personal process to gain ascendency to where I am today, I have learned that my gifting, talents, and abilities have not led me here. It has been my persistent overcoming and tenacious spirit that have brought me to where I am today. The Presence driven life I have created has made me an overcomer and it will do the same for you. You can lose a lot of things in life, but you cannot afford to lose your passion or your persistence. Rise up today with this anointing to finish and prepare to overcome every pain, every perplexity, and every problem so you may obtain the promises of God.

A Presence driven leader has a constant anointing moving him onward and upward. If you are called you cannot quit. If you are chosen there is no throwing in the towel. There is high call of God that thrusts you into the promises of God. What an overcomer goes through would kill the average Christian—but you are not average, you are an overcomer.

Applying the following principles in this chapter will empower you to overcome the challenges in your present and in your future so you may receive all the promises of God for your life. Rise up today. You are a part of an overcoming company!

Quotes for The Overcoming Leader

"Leaders don't find a way, they make one."

"You are not called to manage fear, but to overcome it."

"What you don't resist will persist in your life."

"Long-suffering is a fruit of the Spirit; therefore,
I can tell you if you're full, you can't quit."

"If you're facing Jericho's insurmountable
walls, get ready to bankrupt them."

"What you tolerate will overcome you."

"Overcoming leaders never blend in."

"Take authority over what is against you by releasing the opposite."

"Be not overcome of evil, but overcome evil with good" (Romans 12:21).

"It's time to reset the hour of celebration. Celebration
precedes manifestation … let the party begin!"

"Your promise is the pathway out of your problem."

"Don't be discouraged when God hides you. He
will hide you before He reveals you."

"Uncommon leaders do not co-exist with darkness, they subdue it."

"Breakthrough comes only after you walk through."

"To receive a reward you will need an enemy. David needed Goliath. Your reward awaits you on the other side of the battle."

"You can break your condition by a revelation of your position."

"If ye then be risen with Christ, seek those things which are above, where Christ sitteth on the right hand of God" (Colossians 3:1).

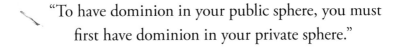

"To have dominion in your public sphere, you must first have dominion in your private sphere."

"Overcoming leaders have little in common with the common."

"How can we take dominion over big stuff if we can't rule over the small stuff?"

"Emotional decisions always bring failure— take dominion of your emotions."

"Learn to master yourself so you can master your world."

"Leaders neglect things that keep them from doing the right things."

"Dominate your thought life or it will dominate you."

"A Presence driven leader's assignment is to reclaim the earth for King Jesus."

"Adversity puts you on your knees, and being on your knees overcomes adversity."

Chapter Nine

A Leader's Honor

The greatest seed a man can ever sow is a seed of honor. All of life flows through the principle of honor. It's not what a man acquires in his life that makes him great, but what he gives away. You'll never know what's in your life until you find the place and people to give it away and share it with.

We live in an era that lacks the principles and the culture of honor—not only outside the church, but within it. The definition of honor in Webster's dictionary is, "The highest degree of respect mingled with awe for the dignity and character of another." Honor recognizes that God has a plan to bring someone in your life so you might become more in God today than you were before you met them. I am personally a composite of the anointings and giftings of many men and women whom God has sent into my life to impart who they are and what they have. I have learned to recognize that God had a plan to bring them into my life so I can be more today than I was before I met them. Everything we become in God is a result of three things; God's Word, our experiences, and another person's influence.

Jesus began His ministry in His home church. The local church should be the breeding ground for great leaders. It is there you receive covering, grow in covenant, learn commitment, and are finally commissioned into your assignment. The first message Jesus taught was on the rewards of honor.

> *And he said, "Verily I say unto you, No prophet is accepted in his own country. But I tell you of a truth, many widows were in Israel in the days of Elijah, when the heaven was shut up three years and six months, when great famine was throughout all the land; But unto none of them was Elijah sent, save unto Sarepta, a city of Sidon, unto a woman that was a widow. And many lepers were in Israel in the time of Elisha the prophet; and none of them was cleansed, saving Naaman the Syrian."*
>
> LUKE 4:24-27

Jesus shared two Old Testament stories concerning honor and the miracles that followed. The first story was about the widow woman in Zarephath. The second story was about Naaman the Syrian. Both honored the prophets: one got health, the other got wealth. The widow woman in Zarephath had been in a three-

and-a-half-year famine. There were many widows in that day, but Elijah was sent to only one of them. She was about to bake her last cake for herself and her son when the Prophet Elijah showed up. After Elijah appeared, the widow woman recognized he was a man of God and honored him. She demonstrated this honor by giving him the last cake that she had prepared for her and her son to eat. Her honor made room for the gift of God in her life. Little did she know her honor of giving her last cake would literally create the first of many cakes.

Honor will put favor on you in the midst of famine. Honor gets the attention of heaven and gives you an open heaven of prosperity. Honor is so powerful it will break the bands of barrenness over your life and give you spiritual immunity in times of recession. Honor will make you recession proof! Honor recognizes the glory on another individual and receives the rewards that follow. If you honor the glory that rests upon a dignitary, that same glory will flow into your life. Honor broke the back of debt on this widow woman's life and released her into a season of more than enough. Honor took the limits off the miracle she needed.

Honor will put favor on you in the midst of famine

There were many lepers in Israel at the time of Elisha, but only Naaman, the captain of the Syrian army, got healed. He was suffering from leprosy when his maid told him about a prophet who could heal him. At first, he was reluctant to believe the prophet, but finally honored the Word of God in Elisha's mouth and received the miracle he needed. Living in the rewards of honor requires instant obedience. Only after following the instructions of Elisha

> **Honor is the catalyst for miracles you need in your life**

did Naaman dip seven times in the Jordan and come forth healed. Honor is the catalyst for miracles you need in your life. Honor will break assignments that have come against your health and prosperity.

On a personal note, I suffered many years from many physical maladies. I truly believe I am alive today as a result of the seeds of honor I sowed during that season. Honor will strengthen and extend your life. If you honor the life sources the Lord has brought into your life, you will see a harvest of miracles that have been prepared for you in heavenly places.

> *But as it is written, Eye hath not seen, nor ear heard, neither have entered into the heart of man, the things which God hath prepared for them that love him.*
>
> 1 CORINTHIANS 2:9

What you see in others you can have if you honor them. The glory in others can be yours if you will honor them. I pray that the quotes of honor in this chapter will challenge you to express honor to others and live a life of honor that will glorify your heavenly Father. Honor must be expressed with acts of kindness, mercy, and love. By demonstrating the principles of honor to the next generation we will honor them with what truly belongs to them. Honor is a choice we must make every day. If we are to see a parade of miracles in our generation, we must create a culture of honor.

The most foolish man is a man without honor. It is important that you remember it is not what or how much you give, it is the honor that your giving comes out of. Start creating a culture of honor today and watch the rewards that follow.

Quotes for A Leader's Honor

"Leaders are kings (walking in authority)
and priests (walking in humility)."

"Leaders of honor make people priority over projects."

"Leaders never magnify their follower's faults, but always magnify their potential."

"When you love and honor your enemies, you
keep your love untainted and pure."

"No leader is born with honor and loyalty, they grow in it."

"As a leader, you will violate others or value
others. Please choose well!"

"Leaders honor life sources so their land and life can be blessed."

**"Honour thy father and thy mother: that thy
days may be long upon the land which the LORD
thy God giveth thee" (Exodus 20:12).**

"How can you lead if you're not under a leader being led?"

"Presence driven leaders become activators and stimulators."

"Leaders of honor never sympathize with sin."

"In a leader's election, loyalty determines
selection (loyalty is royalty)."

"Honor the life-sources the Lord has placed in your life and you will be blessed."

"Honor a dignitary and rewards will follow."

"The greatest gift is a seed of honor."

"Honor will deliver you from the evil of mediocrity."

"Honor succeeds in any environment."

"Honor will put favor on you in the midst of famine."

"Honor will enlarge your borders and carry
you to a place of prosperity."

"The degree of honor a man flows in
determines his level of wisdom."

"Honor is a prerequisite for success."

"Honor is the catalyst for miracles in your life."

"Every leader should honor and esteem the call
of God on their life by demanding the highest
of themselves and others in their care."

**"For I speak to you Gentiles, in as much as I am the apostle
of the Gentiles, I magnify mine office ..." (Romans 11:13).**

"As leaders, our product is people; anything
else is a violation of God's heart."

"Echelon leaders add value to others and never take away."

"The most foolish person in the world is the
man or woman without honor."

"Leaders don't talk down to the next
generation, but build them up."

"Honor breaks curse cycles."

"Familiarity without intimacy always breeds dishonor."

"All life flows out of the principle of honor."

"Honor gives you an audience with God."

"The true essence of the Kingdom is
brokenness, humility, and honor."

"The spirit of honor is a shield protecting you
from the assignments set out against you."

"Honor is the platform for the supernatural in your life."

"Your honor makes you recession proof!"

"Honor invites the Presence of God."

"The anointing you dishonor is the anointing you dispel."

"Honor is the red carpet for the miraculous."

"The glory in others can be yours if you honor them."

"Leaders validate the life of God in men, not the gifts in men."

"The **GREATEST GIFT** is a seed of **HONOR.**"

Chapter Ten

Servant Leadership

True leaders are not self-serving. Those who lead in God's Kingdom know they are servants. Jesus said, "The Spirit of the Lord is upon Me because …" (Luke 4:18). *Because* is a word of purpose. Jesus then lists the five reasons (the *because*) for the anointing upon his life: (1) to preach the gospel to the poor; (2) to heal the brokenhearted; (3) to preach deliverance to the captives, and recovering of sight to the blind; (4) to set at liberty them that are bruised; (5) to preach the acceptable year of the Lord.

> *The Spirit of the Lord is upon Me, because he hath anointed Me to preach the gospel to the poor; He hath sent Me to heal the brokenhearted, to preach deliverance to the captives, and recovering of sight to the blind, to set*

at liberty them that are bruised, to preach the acceptable
year of the Lord.

LUKE 4:18-19

God anoints leaders for a purpose. The anointing upon a leader's life is for service. True leadership serves the Lord by serving their followers.

Abraham is a great example of servant leadership as he armed and trained those under his care. Armed means to empty or pour into. Abraham emptied and poured himself into his followers, reproducing himself and making them servant leaders like himself.

And when Abram heard that his brother was taken captive,
he armed his trained servants, born in his own house, three
hundred and eighteen, and pursued them unto Dan. And
he divided himself against them, he and his servants, by
night, and smote them, and pursued them unto Hobah,
which is on the left hand of Damascus.

GENESIS 14:14-15

Jesus said the highest rank in the Kingdom of God is to be the servant of all. We rule and we reign in our sphere by how we serve people. Being committed to the success of our followers is the greatest way to serve them. Your authority will never go beyond your servanthood. Those Abraham armed and trained were the recipients of the plunder they received while overcoming their enemies. Great rewards will follow those who learn to serve.

> **Your authority will never go beyond your servanthood**

Only when you serve do you have a right to be heard. You will never be a voice to your generation if you never serve your generation.

> *O God, thou hast taught me from my youth: and hitherto have I declared thy wondrous works. Now also when I am old and greyheaded, O God, forsake me not; until I have shewed thy strength unto this generation, and thy power to everyone that is to come.*

> PSALMS 71:17-18

As servant leaders, we are called to bring a piece of God to our generation. David lived out his moment within his generation by serving his generation. Your DNA hardware is one-of-a-kind; God broke the mold when He made you! Without you, there is a piece of God that others will not see. There is something in you that looks so much like God that when you serve others, you manifest Him and reveal that part of God which no one else has.

We never outgrow our servanthood as leaders. Look at Jesus, the model leader who is still serving mankind via the Holy Ghost. Every time you serve mankind, the Spirit of the Son within you is manifesting in pristine servanthood. He leads best who serves the most!

He leads best who serves the most!

One way we serve is by bringing solutions to problems. Our servanthood is manifested by how we treat people. Presence driven leaders treat people like they are the most important people in the world. Loving people is the secret of servanthood. I like to treat people as if they are famous, regardless of whom they are. The nature of a servant will celebrate everyone. It is important to honor dignitaries, but it is just as important to honor, serve, and celebrate the janitor, the waitress, the chef, the mechanic, etc. We are commanded to bestow abundant honor upon the less comely. A true Presence driven servant will find ways every day to build others up.

When I was a young man, I began working for a local florist shop (the one I now own) and I became a new born Christian. The Lord gave me this scripture:

> *And if ye have not been faithful in that which is another man's, who shall give you that which is your own?*
>
> LUKE 16:12

The Lord instructed me to serve the vision of the owner, Mr. Jack Butz, and in return He would see to it that others would serve my vision. Out of 46,000 flower shops at that present time, the flower shop I was working for was in the top one hundred. As I served this man's vision and treated the flower shop like it was my own, I had no idea what was in store for me. Thirty years later my wife and I own the business outright. Mr. Butz turned the flower shop over to us because of how we served his vision. Today others are serving the vision that the Lord has given my wife and me. If you will appropriate them, the principles and patterns of servanthood will work for you just as they have for me. Roll up your sleeves today and start serving your generation and watch the rewards that follow!

Quotes for Servant Leadership

"Leaders solve people's problems. Their solutions open the door to influence."

"If serving is below you, leadership is beyond you."

"Your level of servanthood determines your level of authority."

"If I look for authority, I look for servants."

"Inactivity is immaturity."

"There are two kinds of people: those who wait for things to happen, and those who cause things to happen. Which kind are you?"

"A serving people are a seeing people, when you serve you'll see what most people never see."

"Real authority serves others."

"Leaders teach what they know, but produce who they are."

"Some people talk, some preach, and others lecture. Presence driven leaders change their world."

"Every miracle is in your movement."

"You are the salt of the earth. Salt makes people thirsty. Do you make people thirsty for Jesus?"

"You'll never be remembered by who you are
in this life, but by what you give away."

"Definition of success? SERVANTHOOD."

"When we serve our generation, we live out our moment in time."

"We serve by relating and caring."

"Serving your own desires is the greatest slavery."

"Your gift cluster is what God gives you; acquired
skill is what you do with it. Get to work!"

"Love is not an emotion, but an action."

"Only when you serve do you have a right to be heard."

"Leadership is not a position as much as a responsibility to serve."

"People should never have authority if they're not under authority."

"He leads best who serves the most."

"When your gifts meet the needs of the people,
then the will of God is fulfilled."

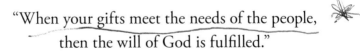

"God sent you here to serve your generation."

"Servant leaders don't fall in love with someone they can live with, but someone they can't live without."

"We serve our generation by bringing a piece of God to it."

"If you want God to do something He has never done before, you'll have to do something that you've never done before."

"It's easier to build strong children than to repair broken men."

"Power is not given to you for you, but to empower someone else."

"Servant leaders go places. People often criticize them for where they are, because they are not willing to pay the price they paid to get there."

"Leadership is not about containing what you have—leaders are a river not a reservoir."

"You will serve who and what you fear."

"**POWER** is given
to **LEADERS** to be
GIVEN AWAY."

Chapter Eleven

The Character of A Leader

We live in a world filled with gifted leaders, but it is rare to find leaders with character. The greatest leaders are great followers who have developed great character. Character is a requirement for the coming moves of God. When Moses smote the rock in disobedience, he was moved by his emotions and not character. The result was that he missed entering the next season of his life.

Character determines the next season of God in your life. God celebrates and promotes character.

God celebrates and promotes character

Our society mirrors the condition of the lack of leaders with character. The present assignment for echelon leaders is to develop character in their own lives and in the lives of their followers.

There are three components to such leadership:

1. Discovery
2. Development
3. Deployment

As leaders we must discover the giftings, callings, anointings, and destinies upon our followers. Then we must develop within them Christ-like character—honor, loyalty, and faithfulness. Only after we help them develop their character can we deploy them by sending them and commissioning them into their sphere of purpose and destiny. To develop such character, we must impart accountability, responsibility, and inevitability within our followers. As emerging leaders, they must become accountable to others and responsible for their actions. Then and only then is success inevitable.

Presence driven leaders create environments for growth, potential, opportunity, and preparation for their followers. It contains a spiritual climate filled with joy, vision, purpose, honor, excellence, revelation, power, and peace. Climates create culture, culture creates belief systems, and the right belief systems create proper behavior and character.

> *He chose David also his servant and took him from the sheepfolds. From **following the ewes great with young** he brought him to feed Jacob his people, and Israel his inheritance. So he fed them **according to the integrity of his heart;** and guided them by the skillfulness of his hands.*
>
> PSALM 78:70-72 (EMPHASIS ADDED)

Many are called, but few choose to go through the training that facilitates leadership: the development of character. David followed the ewes (pregnant sheep). Always follow leaders who are impregnated with purpose, vision, wisdom, and have a Presence driven life. We then see in that David's integrity of heart matched his gift, therefore, his outward gift matched his inward character. This is what we call leading from the inside out.

There is an urgency in the heart of God to reveal Kingdom assignments in this present day. To fulfill that assignment it will take more than gifting, talent, and ability; it will take Christ-like character. As character is restored to this new breed of leaders, the image of God will once again be restored in the earth. The word *likeness* means gifting, talent, and ability. The image of God is the character and nature of God.

> *This is the book of the generations of Adam. In the day that God created man, in the likeness of God made he him.*
>
> GENESIS 5:1

Adam was created in the likeness and image of God. After the fall, Adam lost the image or the character of God, and had only the likeness of God. From the fall of mankind, God still created man in His likeness, but no longer in His image. We see this today where man has great gifting and ability, but little character. Jesus has come to restore the image and character of God back to mankind.

> *Who being the brightness of his glory, and the express image of his person, and upholding all things by the word of his*

*power, when he had by himself purged our sins, sat down
on the right hand of the Majesty on high.*

HEBREWS 1:3

*For the Son of man is come to seek and to save that which
was lost.*

LUKE: 19:10 (EMPHASIS ADDED)

This was the Son of God's mission statement: to come and restore that which was lost—the character of God. The Lord is restoring His image back in the earth through Presence driven leadership. All men are born with gifting, talent, and ability, but lack the image and character of God. If we are to see God's image manifested in the midst of a wicked and perverse generation, His image must be restored through the leaders of our day.

Jesus was the express image of God. Or we could say that Jesus expressed the image of His Father. Jesus was the Father's highest thought expressed in the earth. We are to be the same in this world. You are to express the character and nature of God in the world in which you live.

Jesus expressed the image of His Father

Holiness is equivalent to character. Holiness means, "I am His!" The Bible tells us, "Without holiness no man shall see the Lord" (Hebrews 12:14). I state it this way, "Without holiness and character, no man will see the Lord in me." The next dimension of glory is earmarked by character. You never determine your level of character in the good times, but in the bad times.

Resistance in the time of temptation is a sign of true character. We are not born with developed character, we grow into it. Gifts are given, but character is grown. I have learned as a Presence driven leader to spend more time working on myself than working on others. The best way I can serve others is by allowing the Lord to work Christ-like character in me.

> **Resistance in the time of temptation is a sign of true character**

Fiery circumstances are the greatest refining tools of character. Presence driven leaders never run from the fire, but walk through the fires knowing that greater Christ-like character will be developed in them and lead them into a greater season of glory. Character means doing the right thing even when no one is watching. My prayer is that the quotes that follow will help develop Christ-like character within your life.

Quotes for The Character of A Leader

"Character is greater than talent and gifting."

"Poor companionships create poor character."

"The curse of insecurity is the death of authority."

"Leaders shift their followers from negatives to positives."

"Presence driven leaders celebrate character above talent."

"Leaders don't expect from others what they
aren't willing to do themselves."

"What you don't resist will persist in your life."

"Leadership sometimes means going in alone."

"Leaders with confidence are never on the defense."

"Leaders know gifts are given but character is grown."

"Leaders work more on their own faults than other's faults."

"If you can't handle correction you can't lead."

"Real leaders who have real character know
how to handle bad behavior."

"Leaders make decisions based upon character and principles,
not on opinions and emotions (which always lead to failure)."

"True character is what a man thinks about all day long."

"The leader's golden rule: If you say something,
please have the life to back it up."

"Pressure on the outside brings out the conqueror on the inside."

"What doesn't kill you makes you stronger."

"The more you go through, the more dangerous you are."

"A man with an opinion is no match for
a man with an experience."

"Are you having attacks or just an inconvenient moment?"

"What you fear you will empower. Where you put your faith you will empower. Choose well."

"A healthy leader has a healthy family, that is a leader's top priority."

"A man with character stands in the fire, a man without character will run from the fire."

"Don't allow your gift to take you where your character can't keep you."

"Presence driven leaders do the right things when others are not around because they know God is."

"The famous last words of a weak ineffective leader, 'Well, I've always done it this way.'"

"Quit just talking about Jesus and show them Jesus—it is show and tell time."

"A virtuous man or woman strikes fear in the bowels of hell."

"When your character matches your assignment, convergence hits. Everything comes looking for you: people, resources, and wealth."

"Murmuring and complaining set limits on your life."

"Character precedes your next realm of glory."

"It's nice to be nice, but better to be honest."

"You must aspire to be a great person before you become a great leader."

"Inward purity is imperative before there is outward power!"

"And Joshua said unto the people, sanctify yourselves: for tomorrow the LORD will do wonders among you" (Joshua 3:5).

"When a leader is wrapped up in himself, he makes a very small package."

"It's nice to be important, but it is more important to be nice."

"If you are unappreciated by fake people, it's because you're too real for them."

"Leaders are believers, not feelers."

"Always build out of strengths, not weaknesses."

"Every leader has two kinds of people around them: people who want to kiss them, and people who want to kill them."

"Behind every excuse is just the lack of desire."

"Your character is revealed by the friends you keep."

"Leading is never what you do, but who you are."

"Leaders do not care where they come in the pecking order as long as what needs to get done happens."

"Integrity means doing the right thing when no one is watching."

"Leaders with real character have grace for others bad behavior."

"People leave you because they can't be you."

"Every word you speak has prophetic implications."

"Leaders with Christ-like character will cause people to run to them or from them."

"Leaders lead in love. People are priority over projects."

"The Lord grades His leaders on attitude."

"One bad decision can erase a lifetime of good decisions."

"Today's fruit, is a result of yesterday's seed."

"Leaders never complain about getting older, some people don't have that privilege."

"Bad company will corrupt good character."

"Never address what you're not willing to roll up your sleeves and change."

"Before you lead corporately, you must be whole individually."

"You know an uncommon leader by death to his self-life."

"Every leader must deal with their personal control issues if they are to reach the next level."

"A leader's mind is a garden: pull out the weeds, kill the snakes, and water the fruit."

"You must be the change that you desire to see in your world."

"Relationships that rob you of your strength are extremely toxic and need to be severed. Cut them off before they take you out."

"Don't let your gift take you where your character can't keep you."

"**CHARACTER** is given to you by **GOD**, while **REPUTATION** is given to you by **MAN**."

Chapter Twelve

A Leader of Excellence

Let the righteous smite me; it shall be a kindness: and let him reprove me; it shall be an excellent oil, which shall not break my head: for yet my prayer also shall be in their calamities.

PSALM 141:5

The psalmist tells us there is an anointing of excellence reserved for us. The earmark of a Presence driven leader is the oil of excellence. Excellence is not a skill, but an attitude. No one is rewarded for being average. I have never promoted or given raises to my employees who are average. Excellence is giving the best you have with what you have been given. Excellence is more than an action, it's a lifestyle. I have always endeavored to treat my

Excellence is giving the best you have with what you have been given

employees the way I want them to treat my customers. This is how I built a business of excellence.

Excellence is doing common things in an uncommon way. It has a way of celebrating everyone under your care. Jesus said to go the extra mile, "If a man compels you to go one mile then go two" (Matthew 5:41). Herein lies the secret to excellence. An uncommon leader will go above and beyond the call of duty because they have the oil of excellence upon their life. Excellence will always under promise and over deliver.

I therefore, the prisoner of the Lord, beseech you that ye walk worthy of the vocation wherewith ye are called.

EPHESIANS 4:1

We should always require excellence of ourselves and everyone under our care. The oil of excellence on a leader will not tolerate lethargy, unbelief, procrastination, or the easy way out. Jesus is the pattern Presence driven leader. He had a more excellent ministry. Let us follow the pattern Son, Jesus Christ, and do the absolute best with what the Lord has given us. The Spirit of excellence will cause you to excel in everything the Lord has assigned you to do.

As you move in the oil of excellence, you can expect extraordinary things to happen in your life. An excellent Spirit prepares you to do something so huge, so awesome, and so massive you don't have time to play around. Excellence will set you up for promotion, opportunities, and prosperity. When a Presence driven leader has a Spirit of excellence they stand out in the crowd.

Then this Daniel was preferred above the presidents and princes, because an excellent spirit was in him; and the king thought to set him over the whole realm.

DANIEL 6:3

Daniel had a more excellent spirit which promoted him and made him prosperous in the midst of a pagan society. Excellence will empower you to come out of the lowest places and rise to the top of your sphere. Daniel came out of the lion's pit to prosper in the king's palace as a result of his excellent spirit.

Excellence will empower you to come out of the lowest places and rise to the top of your sphere

He delivereth and rescueth, and he worketh signs and wonders in heaven and in earth, who hath delivered Daniel from the power of the lions. So this Daniel prospered in the reign of Darius, and in the reign of Cyrus the Persian.

DANIEL 6:27-28

When the oil of excellence saturates a Presence driven leader it sends a signal to heaven that they are ready for more. The blessings of God are not accidental. They require the oil of excellence. May the oil of excellence empower you to excel in all that God has called you to do!

Quotes for The Leader of Excellence

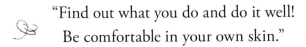

"Find out what you do and do it well!
Be comfortable in your own skin."

"Presence driven leaders think differently, praise differently,
live differently, talk differently, and give differently."

"What right do you have to hold back the gifts you have and the gift you are?"

"Just being a Christian will not get you a job or
keep you on the job; character, honor, excellence,
passion, attitude, and commitment will."

"Your gift cluster is what God gives you,
acquired skill is what you do with it."

"Leaders have a low tolerance for lethargy."

"Leaders know that responsibility is the price for greatness."

"When leaders don't hold up high standards, there are no standards."

"The difference between excellence and
average is real and noticeable."

"If there are not three people who want to
be like you, you must work harder."

 "Excellence is not a skill but an attitude—a mindset."

"Excellent leaders never use duct-tape for a temporary fix, they repair and mend things well."

"God doesn't bless you for being a leader. He rewards you for diligence and excellence."

"Real leaders are desperate for what's real and what works."

"What defines you is not how you fall, but how you rise after you fall."

"Then this Daniel was preferred above the presidents and princes, because an excellent spirit [was] in him; and the king thought to set him over the whole realm" (Daniel 6:3).

"Leaders leave the room a better place."

"Leaders of excellence are a dream to some people, but a nightmare to others."

"Leaders name and nature their environment so no one else can."

"Leaders of excellence are offensive minded, never defensive."

"One good decision can erase a lifetime of bad decisions."

"Be authentic, be real, be you! No one can do it like you, say it like you, or reflect it like you."

"We compete in the marketplace by service and excellence."

"You only have one chance to make a lasting impression. Make it in EXCELLENCE!"

"You can't lead the people if you live below
the standard of the people."

**"Seest thou a man diligent in his business? he
shall stand before kings; he shall not stand
before mean men" (Proverbs 22:29).**

"Presence driven leaders never replace
excellence for average in their life."

"No one is rewarded for being average."

"Leaders with excellence build a level of
expectation for their followers."

"If you're called to be the best and you settle
for good, that makes you fair."

"Excellence will empower you to come out from the lowest places and soar to the highest places."

"Delayed gratification is important if you don't
want to settle for less than God's best."

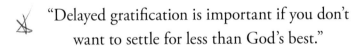

"Neglect the things that stop you from doing the right things."

"When you walk in excellence and refuse to be
common, you will probably offend the common."

"The greatness in you reveals the smallness in others. Refuse
to think small, the GREATER ONE IS IN YOU!"

"Leaders refuse to allow average to replace excellence in their life."

Chapter Thirteen

The Favor
of A Leader

Everything God does in the earth has the face of a man or woman on it. This new breed of leader must first be fashioned by God before they are favored by God. The Lord has a way of handling His emerging leaders. He is the potter and we are the clay. He will carve a leader out with His own hands, preparing them for greatness. He has a way of luring us into our wilderness, much like he did with David and Moses, to fashion us (as He did them) for a position of favor. Once Moses had been fashioned he was mantled with such favor that God said, "You shall be like a god unto Pharaoh" (Exodus 7:1).

After Moses was fashioned and favored by God, he was sent in the place of God so that when Pharaoh saw Moses he saw God.

Such favor is an incredible force. When you are mantled with God's favor, when devils face you, they face the God in you.

Favor is a powerful influence, so much that people become jealous of the gifts you have and the gift you are. This favor makes people jealous of the God you serve!

Every good gift and every perfect gift is from above, and cometh down from the Father of lights.

JAMES 1:17

You are God's good and perfect gift sent from the Father into your world. Favor is nothing more and nothing less than God's incredible influence resting upon your life. It is an incredible force that is so attractive it entices others to bless you and be committed to your success. The psalmist said that there is a set time for the Lord to favor you.

Thou shalt arise, and have mercy upon Zion: for the time to favour her, yea, the set time, is come.

PSALM 102:13

This set time shows up suddenly when preparation and destiny converge.

And let us not be weary in well doing: for in due season we shall reap, if we faint not.

GALATIANS 6:9

The Greek word for *due* in this passage of scripture means "personal and private." The Greek word for *season* is *kairos* meaning "special occasions, a set time and opportune time." The Lord makes everything beautiful in His time. There is a set time that God will personally favor you. This is when the extraordinary favor of God invades the ordinary. This set time is an epiphany. An epiphany is when what God has always known about you becomes apparent to you and everyone in your world. It's when your season of preparation runs into your season of manifestation.

There is a set time that God will personally favor you

The favor of God rested upon Joseph so much that everywhere he landed God blessed. Joseph's life is a wonderful picture of one that has been fashioned and favored by God.

And the Lord was with Joseph, and he was a prosperous man; and he was in the house of his master the Egyptian.

GENESIS 39:2

But the Lord was with Joseph, and shewed him mercy, and gave him favour in the sight of the keeper of the prison.

GENESIS 39:21

The Lord blessed Potiphar's house for the sake of Joseph. All that Potiphar had was blessed as result of the favor upon Joseph. When Joseph descended into the prison house, scripture says that the Lord was with him and showed him mercy and gave him favor in the sight of the prison keeper. Favor is a direct result of God being with us. His Presence within our lives manifests in favor. Favor comes to make you look good. Favor is the kiss of heaven upon your life!

This incredible favor was given to the children of Israel when preparing for the Exodus out of Egypt.

And the children of Israel did according to the word of Moses; and they borrowed of the Egyptians jewels of silver, and jewels of gold, and raiment: and the Lord gave the people favour in the sight of the Egyptians, so that they lent unto them such things as they required. And they spoiled the Egyptians.

EXODUS 12:35-36

The Egyptians gave the Israelites great wealth that God would ultimately use for Kingdom advancement.

Favor is God's promise of success. Favor comes to you when you are in the most unfavorable circumstances. How would anyone see favor without a backdrop of unfavorable circumstances? Where there is favor there will always be a foe. The Lord put favor on Joseph in the most unfavorable places. God will put you in the most horrific circumstances to show you and everyone around you that He is with you and for you!

> **How would anyone see favor without a backdrop of unfavorable circumstances?**

Favor only comes to those who are on divine assignment.

And the angel came in unto her, and said, Hail, thou that art highly favoured, the Lord is with thee: blessed art thou among women. And when she saw him, she was troubled at his saying, and cast in her mind what manner of salutation this should be. And the angel said unto her, "Fear not, Mary: for thou hast found favour with God."

LUKE 1:28-30

Once Mary was impregnated with her assignment, the angel told her she was highly favored and had found favor in the sight of God. We were told that Jesus had favor with God and man. This is the double portion anointing we need to fulfill our divine destinies. We have always had favor with God, but to fulfill our destiny in Christ we must also receive favor from man. This is a result of God's preparations in our lives. God honors Presence driven leaders with favor. When He sees tenacity, persistence, perseverance, faithfulness, and your willingness, you can expect favor to come nipping at your heels. When it is your set time to be favored as a leader, I don't care if 1,000 people say no—if God says yes then it's yes.

If you have been in a season of preparation, your preparation is not being wasted. Be encouraged, a set time to favor you is coming! Be not weary in well doing for in due season you will reap a harvest if you don't quit. Remember God makes everything beautiful in His time.

My prayer is that the following quotes will fashion you and prepare you for the favor that will follow.

Quotes for The Favor of A Leader

"We are never to pursue success, we pursue God's favor."

"Favor is the promise of success."

"The greatest resource a leader can have is favor."

"Presence driven leaders pursue faithfulness because favor always finds faithfulness."

"The greatest asset of a leader is not their charisma or gifting, but their influence."

"Opportunity favors prepared minds."

"Your gift may not always be accepted by others, but will be rewarded by God."

"And the LORD shall guide thee continually, and satisfy thy soul in drought, and make fat thy bones: and thou shalt be like a watered garden, and like a spring of water, whose waters fail not" (Isaiah58:11).

"Favor is God's yes and amen backing your dream."

"The favor upon your life is greater than your need."

"The JOY of the NEW will always overtake the heartache of the old!"

"God will outdo what He has done in your past. He always outdoes Himself!"

"Leaders are fashioned by God before they are favored by God."

"For thou, LORD, wilt bless the righteous; with favour wilt thou compass him as with a shield" (Psalm 5:12).

 "The more enemies that come against you, the more God will raise you up."

"Favor gravitates leaders to the top of their sphere."

"Great favor always attracts great opposition."

"Divine favor shows up when you solve problems and create solutions."

"Favor makes you stand out in the crowd."

"God always has someone to accept you when others reject you."

"Your greatest resource in God's Kingdom is FAVOR."

"For the LORD God is a sun and shield: the LORD will give grace and glory: no good thing will he withhold from them that walk uprightly" (Psalm 84:11).

"**FAVOR** is a direct result of **GOD** being **WITH US.**"

Chapter Fourteen

The Prosperous Leader

The uncommon leader will always create uncommon wealth because the uncommon leader is an uncommon giver. For years I decreed I would be the wealthiest man in my city. After many years the Lord spoke to my spirit and said, "Son I don't want you to be the wealthiest man in the city, but the most giving man in your city." Presence driven leaders get a vision of how much they can give away, not how much they can get.

Prosperity in a Presence driven leader is not accidental. There has never been one dollar fall from heaven. Wealth creation is not magical, nor is it a Kingdom lottery. It is a precise application of patterns and principles that produce certain results.

But thou shalt remember the Lord thy God: for it is He that giveth thee power to get wealth, that He may establish his covenant which He sware unto thy fathers, as it is this day.

DEUTERONOMY 8:18

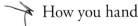

Innate in every believer is the power to create wealth. The Lord does not give us wealth, but the power to create wealth. What are some of these powers? They are vision, skill, wisdom, stewardship, character, excellence, and networking … just to name a few.

How you handle your money is how God handles you.

- Achan stole the first fruits that were reserved for God. Because of his greed, he aborted his inheritance and forfeited the promises of God.

- King Saul mismanaged the spoils after defeating the Amalekites. Because of his disobedience, he surrendered the kingdom to a shepherd boy.

Money always determines the next season in your life.

- Judas, who had been the Lord's treasurer for three and half years, mishandled the Lord's money. Because of his lack of stewardship he missed the next season for which he had been chosen.

- Ananias and Sapphira mishandled the tithe. Because they lied to the Holy Ghost about their money, they did not transition into the apostolic season.

None of these individuals fulfilled their destiny. How you handle money is how God handles you.

How you manage your wealth will qualify you as an uncommon leader. Uncommon leaders have a spirit of generosity. You will never be a custodian of wealth without a spirit of generosity. It is impossible to have the nature of God and not be generous. The Father so loved the world He gave out of His generous heart. Love was expressed by giving the greatest gift, His only begotten Son. Uncommon leaders dismantle greed and exchange it for a mantle of generosity.

You will never be a custodian of wealth without the spirit of generosity

Money never makes you, it only unmasks you. If you are greedy you will become more miserly, but if you are a giver you will become more generous. This is the power of increase. What restricts the supply of wealth is the failure to give away. Uncommon leaders don't look for where to get money, but where they can give it away. The acquisition of large sums of money never changes anyone for the good or bad, it only strengthens who they already are. If you are struggling to find provision, I submit, you need a vision of where you can release it.

All prosperity must be attached to purpose. This was the problem with the prosperity movement of the 80s and 90s. You can only produce after your purpose. The Father only creates resources for the work He has commissioned you to do.

Jesus talks about wealth in two-thirds of the parables. The Bible has a lot to say about wealth creation. You cannot fulfill the call of God without it. Matthew 25 shares the story of the parable of the talents where the master gave his goods to three servants. Our Heavenly Master is the possessor and we are the stewards. The goods represent the power to get wealth. Once again, God doesn't give us wealth, but the power to get wealth. One servant was given five talents, another two, and yet another one. Just like these three men, you presently have all God can trust you with—your money measures you. The Lord will not give you more than what you can manage. The servants with five and two increased what they were given by doubling it. The servant with one hoarded what he had and lost it.

Here we see how the Lord increases what we have increased. We see the principle that what we maintain in life we will lose. Maintenance is dangerous. God never blesses the lack, but the increase. If God blessed lack there would be no poor people in the world. The reward for these two servants for what they had been given was rulership and authority over two cities. In the coming moves of the Spirit, those who master their money and learn the principles of increase will have authority over cities and be given Kingdom resources to fulfill their destiny. Managing your wealth qualifies you for greater leadership and rulership.

Managing your wealth qualifies you for greater leadership

Under Moses' administration, which prefigured the Kingdom of God, he provided resources for three million people. Even Manasseh, the smallest tribe, prospered under his leadership. In the coming moves of the Spirit we will see that

Presence driven leaders, much like Moses, will become custodians of large sums of wealth to administrate God's purposes in their lives and in the lives of their followers.

The spirit of consumption is the greatest killer of a leader. It will keep them from becoming a wealth builder. When you dismantle greed and exchange it with a mantle of generosity, you are then ready to subdue and occupy the Kingdom of mammon.

The Kingdom of God begins with generosity. Presence driven leaders do not look for provision, but learn to release it and thus become a channel of prosperity. Quit looking for how you will get money and start looking where to pour it out. As you learn to steward money properly, you will be prepared to become God's wallet.

> *That I may cause those that love me to inherit substance; and I will fill their treasures.*
>
> PROVERBS 8:21

In this passage we see a promise to those who love the Lord that they will inherit substance and He will fill their treasures.

Intimacy with God will keep you from being intimate with your wallet. A Presence driven life will keep the principle of prosperity in the proper perspective. Intimacy with the Lord connects you to God's Kingdom supply. Intimacy is the key to open up the Kingdom's storehouse.

The Apostle James said the rich have heaped up treasures for these last days (James 5:3). The world is facilitating riches until Kingdom men and woman are prepared to handle it. Today's preparation determines tomorrow's wealth. It is August as I write this book, and my greenhouses are growing poinsettias. No one is calling our store and asking for poinsettias, but we know that they will bring great profit in December. What you prepare for will show up in your future. I call this the greenhouse effect. You must refuse to miss your next season because you are unprepared. God gives seed to the sower not the taker. Start creating wealth today by sowing who you are and what you have. Apply the following quotes in this chapter and watch the power to create wealth come alive.

Quotes for The Prosperous Leader

"Your seed doesn't relate to recession."

"You'll never live beyond your giving."

"It's not what you acquire in life, but what you give away that matters."

"A leader's love is measured by their giving."

"Echelon leaders know how to seize the moment or miss the blessing."

"You'll never know what's in you until you find the place to give it away."

"Maintenance is dangerous business, if you don't expand what you have you'll lose it."

"If you don't leave a better world for your
children, you have failed in life."

"Always be thankful for success, never apologize for it."

"The most joyful people in the world don't have the best
of everything, but make the best of everything."

"Provision is only promised at the place of your assignment."

"Lack can corrupt the purposes of God quicker than prosperity."

"The best way to take vengeance on hell is massive success."

"Your seed today puts an expiration date on your present season and opens doors to your next season."

"Winners are more than willing to do what losers are not."

"It's within your ability to give your absolute best."

"Your next level of living will require a new level of giving."

"To give is to live!"

"God doesn't bless you for being a Christian,
He rewards diligence and passion."

"People who solve problems go from being the tail to the head."

"People want a harvest without sowing a seed,
that's a violation of God's Kingdom order."

"Money doesn't have a mind of its own until it gets into your hand."

"Wealth for God's service is the proper approach for seeking wealth."

"When your internal and external state aligns with one another, then you're marked for success."

"Let me offer this advice: love what you do and the money will come nipping at your heels."

"Your giving reveals your heart."

"Generosity is not the size of your bank account, but the size of your heart."

"Quit looking at the limitations and start looking for His miraculous provision."

"If you want a harvest you have to sow something, if you want a promise you have to overcome something, and if you want an inheritance you have to be someone."

"Wealthy mindsets thrive while poverty mindsets survive."

"There is always a process before provision."

"Money only unmasks what's already in your heart."

"Why should the Lord give you more wealth, wisdom, anointing, gifts and power if you haven't given away what you have?"

"The amount of wealth you create is determined by the size of the problem you solve."

"Increasing your GIVING increases your LIVING."

"If you want money alone, you're not ready for it, but if you want to change your world then money has need of you."

"Stewardship grants you the privilege of greatness."

"In God's economy, impossible is only a word!"

"Uncommon wealth visits uncommon people."

"Violent sowing prepares the way for violent reaping."

"God will never prosper immobility. GET MOVING!"

"How you handle money is how God handles you."

"Are you possessed by wealth or Kingdom advancement?"

"For every reason you feel you should not be blessed, I'll give you 1,000 reasons why you should."

"The LORD God of your fathers make you a thousand times so many more as ye are, and bless you, as He hath promised you!" (Deuteronomy 1:11).

"Jesus has provided a solution to every problem we face, it is our job to appropriate the provision."

"The acquisition of large sums of money never change a man for good or for evil, it only strengthens who he already is."

"Blessed are those who expect nothing, they will never be disappointed. Raise your expectation!"

"The power to create wealth is not outside of you, but resident within you. Rise up and release it!"

"Leaders get family right, spirit right, money right, and their walk right."

"Poverty mentalities continually curse themselves."

 "You have to sow where you want to go."

"Fame and fortune will chase Presence driven leaders, but we never chase them."

"Receiving without giving is shoplifting."

"The life you have is not yours to possess, but it is a life to be given away."

"You will never have a need as long as you have a seed."

"It's your season to persist in prosperity."

Chapter Fifteen

The Successful Leader

Success without successors is failure in disguise. If you look for success, you don't look at the leaders, but into the lives of those who follow them. True success will breed successors. Four hundred men watched David kill a giant and pursued his leadership anointing into the cave of Adullam. It was there he reproduced himself within his followers, creating a military might. David's commitment to their success empowered them to be great leaders. Successful leaders honor, serve, and empower their followers.

When a leader goes up he should take his followers with him, this is true success. When David was promoted as king he took his followers with him.

When Jesus ascended to the throne the disciples also ascended into their apostolic assignments. As Jesus was elevated into His new seat of authority, He lifted His followers up into their new place of authority. This is successful leadership.

> *So then after the Lord had spoken unto them, he was received up into heaven, and sat on the right hand of God. And they went forth, and preached everywhere, the Lord working with them, and confirming the word with signs following. Amen.*

MARK 16:19-20

Saul was a weak and anemic leader and became jealous of his successor, David. Saul was David's leader, but he tried to pin him to the wall with his spear, limiting his progress and promotion. Insecure leaders will always restrict their followers from progress and promotion.

True leadership always brings their followers to new levels. There was a man who had been carried and let down daily at the temple, at the gate called Beautiful. As he had been let down there daily, so have many leaders let down their followers. But let's look at the leadership of Peter and John who went up together to the temple to worship and there encountered this lame man who had been let down by the leadership of that day:

> *Now Peter and John went up together into the temple at the hour of prayer, being the ninth hour. And a certain man lame from his mother's womb was carried, whom they laid daily at the gate of the temple which is called Beautiful, to*

The Successful Leader | 131

ask alms of them that entered into the temple; who seeing Peter and John about to go into the temple asked for alms.

And Peter, fastening his eyes upon him with John, said, "Look on us."

And he gave heed unto them, expecting to receive something of them. Then Peter said, "Silver and gold have I none; but such as I have give I thee: In the name of Jesus Christ of Nazareth rise up and walk."

And he took him by the right hand, and lifted him up: and immediately his feet and ankle bones received strength. And he leaping up stood, and walked, and entered with them into the temple, walking, and leaping, and praising God. And all the people saw him walking and praising God.

ACTS 3:1-9

Peter reached down and lifted this man up out of his lame position. Successful leaders do not go down to where their followers are, but instead reach down and lift them up to where they are. As this man's feet and ankles received strength, get the picture of how successful leaders strengthen the walk of their followers. This man went from a lame to a leap! Successful leaders invest in people when they are down. Before you can leap into destiny, you must first learn to walk. It will take a successful leader to strengthen your walk so you can fulfill your destiny. The earmark of a successful leader is that they strengthen their followers to leap into destiny.

Successful leaders strengthen the walk of their followers

The true essence of a successful leader is found in their anointing. When my anointing and influence makes others work harder, step up, rise up, move out, make changes, and bring encouragement, then I am successful. The proof of a successful leader is their ability to conquer the temptations and horrific circumstances in their follower's lives. Presence driven leaders carry an anointing that will lead their followers into a successful and prosperous life. Successful leaders impart their anointing, gifts, visions, and strength into their followers. You can identify a successful leader because they are the ones who will put vision in you.

Successful leaders impart their anointings, gifts, visions, and strength into their followers

The Lord is presently raising up Presence driven leaders who are not seeking others to be committed to their success, but are committed to the success of their followers. As leaders, if we don't leave a better world for our followers we have failed. So many people equate success with education, wealth, charisma, gifting, or popularity. True success is found in a Presence driven leader who can use their anointing to bring change to their followers and empower them to be the best they can be in God.

May the following quotes in this chapter reconfigure your mindsets to create a lifestyle of successful leadership.

The Successful Leader Quotes

"Failure is a great teacher that prepares you for success."

"If you're asking God for a common life,
you're asking Him not to use you."

"Intellect is not the answer to success, character is."

"Despising small beginnings is a violation of
success in God's Kingdom order."

"True success is turning followers into leaders and leaders into world changers."

"When a leader sees success as influence, they
are ready to change their world."

"Have you become an overnight success? Sorry it's not God."

"Successful leaders hang out with dangerous
people, not safe people."

"Once you are delivered from foolish
people, you are ready for success."

"You were chosen in Him before the foundation of the
world, therefore you are preprogrammed for success."

"It took your whole life to get here today, Enjoy it to the fullest!"

**"This is the day which the LORD hath made; we
will rejoice and be glad in it" (Psalms 118:24).**

"Figure out what you do well and do it every day."

"Being at the right place at the right time won't make you successful unless you're prepared for it."

"Replace the idea of surviving with the goal of succeeding."

"Blessed is the man that endureth temptation: for when he is tried, he shall receive the crown of life, which the Lord hath promised to them that love him" (James 1:12).

"Leaders first value themselves so they can value others (love your neighbor as yourself)."

"Leaders create a rhythm in life for success."

"Successful leaders are like the common cold, get close enough to them and you'll catch it and spread it to others."

"Leaders know survival comes before success."

"Problems are not real problems to leaders who are graced in that department."

"Leaders are only successful when their followers are successful."

"Leaders are shifters that shift others from negatives to positives."

"People only see the package, but never open you up to see your packing power!"

"The birth of function is the death of dysfunction."

"Aspiring for greatness? Then don't settle for a mediocre life."

"You have to put a miracle in motion— it's called the WORKING of miracles."

"Leaders recognize that success is found in quality not quantity."

"Public success is a result of your private life with the Lord."

"Success is when your sphere operates like you when you're not there."

"Successful people do whatever they do with all their might."

And keep the charge of the Lord thy God, to walk in his ways, to keep his statutes, and his commandments, and his judgments, and his testimonies, as it is written in the law of Moses, that thou mayest prosper in all that thou doest, and whithersoever thou turnest thyself" (1 Kings 2:3).

"Success is written in your DNA."

"Success shows up to people who are too busy to look for it! P.S. Gotta run, I'm very busy!"

"Loving people is the secret to success."

"Real success is being Christ-like."

"True success is found when you are locked in eternity while living in time."

"I don't have time to waste with thoughts in my head that God does not have in His."

"Success is not success if your ego is attached to it."

"True **LEADERS**
replace the goal
of **SURVIVING**
with the goal of
SUCCEEDING."

Meet the Author

Dr. Mark Kauffman

Being passionately involved in both business and ministry, Dr. Mark Kauffman possesses a unique ability to equip and train leaders. He links the idea of prosperity to a God-given plan that will foster a culture of honor and advance the Kingdom of God in the earth. His heart is to see the body of Christ demonstrate the nature and ministry of the Lord Jesus, thus fulfilling their designed destiny.

Dr. Kauffman received his Doctorate of Divinity from Tabernacle Bible School and University and his ministry experience expands over 28 years. He is the founder and executive pastor of Jubilee Ministries International City Church located in New Castle, Pennsylvania.

Since 1987, he has successfully owned and operated Butz Flowers, Gifts and Home Décor, the second oldest florist in the United States and ranked in the top 100 of 30,000 florists nationwide. He is also CEO of Destiny Developers, Kingdom Broadcasting Network Studios (KBN), and the Christian Chamber of Commerce of Western Pennsylvania (CCWP). CCCWP equips, trains, and commissions men and women into the marketplace influencing their sphere with the Kingdom of Heaven.

Mark has been happily married for 28 years to Dr. Jill Kauffman, who works tirelessly alongside him to see the Kingdom of God advance, therefore, impacting generations. Together they have three sons—Anthony, Ryan, and Christian Mark,—and three grandchildren.

To learn more about the Christian Chamber of Commerce of Western Pennsylvania (CCWP), please visit:

www.cccwp.us

To connect with Dr. Mark, please visit:

www.thepresencedrivenlife.com